333.91
004

TITLE V 2002

35982

S0-ABC-893

Marjory Stoneman Douglas

Guardian of the 'Glades

KIERAN DOHERTY

TWENTY-FIRST CENTURY BOOKS
BROOKFIELD, CONNECTICUT

Cover photograph courtesy of Corbis (© Kevin Fleming) and Tom Stack & Associates (© Therisa Stack)

Photographs courtesy of Archives and Special Collections, University of Miami Library, Coral Gables, Florida: pp. 12, 18, 52, 72, 83, 90; Corbis: p. 15 (© Kevin Fleming); Florida State Archives: p. 17; Wellesley College Archives: pp. 28, 34; Brown Brothers: pp. 31, 63; Getty Images: pp. 49 (© Hulton/Archive), 66 (© Hulton/Archive); Tom Stack & Associates: p. 101 (© Therisa Stack); Historical Museum of Southern Florida: p. 107; © Miami Herald: pp. 112, 129; AP/Wide World Photos: p. 126.

Library of Congress Cataloging-in-Publication Data
Doherty, Kieran.
Marjory Stoneman Douglas : guardian of the 'glades / Kieran Doherty.
p. cm.
Summary: A biography of the Florida environmental activist whose efforts on behalf of the Everglades have resulted in the protection and revitalization of that area.
Includes bibliographical references and index.
ISBN 0-7613-2371-6 (lib. bdg.)
1. Douglas, Marjory Stoneman—Juvenile literature. 2. Conservationists—Florida—Biography—Juvenile literature. 3. Nature conservation—Florida—Everglades—Juvenile literature. [1. Douglas, Marjory Stoneman. 2. Conservationists. 3. Nature conservation—Florida—Everglades. 4. Everglades (Fla.)] I. Title.
QH31.D645 D65 2002   333.91'8'0975939092—dc21   2002004977

Published by Twenty-First Century Books
A Division of The Millbrook Press, Inc.
2 Old New Milford Road
Brookfield, Connecticut 06804

Contents

To Jack Furet for all his help...
and in memory of Carol Morton Furet.

Introduction

I saw Marjory Stoneman Douglas very briefly in 1984 or 1985. At that time I was working as a freelance writer in South Florida, covering a meeting of the Miami-Dade County Commission. Suddenly, the large, crowded room where the meeting was being held fell silent as a woman rose from her seat near the front of the room and began to address the county commissioners. As this tiny woman wearing an oversized straw hat spoke, I could hear those close to me whispering her name. "Marjory Douglas . . . Marjory Stoneman Douglas. . . ."

Of course, I knew her name. I knew what most people who lived in Florida knew then and know today: that she was a famous author who wrote a book about the Everglades and then turned her attention to saving it from encroaching civilization.

I don't, in all honesty, recall what she spoke of that day. I do recall being impressed by the impact her presence in the room had on those around me. As time passed and I saw her name in the newspaper, always connected with some effort to protect the Everglades or stop some ill-advised attempt to change Florida's natural landscape, I became more and more aware of her tireless energy and willingness to stand up against seemingly overwhelming foes. Over time, I became more interested in her life, wondering what made her such a passionate conservationist.

It was not until Douglas's death in 1998 that I began to think seriously of writing her biography. What I discovered amazed me. I found that there was much more to Marjory Stoneman Douglas than her life as, in her words, a "writing woman," or, indeed, her work as a protector of the 'Glades.

I found that Douglas had to overcome seemingly unbeatable odds—including a sad, almost tragic childhood and a disastrous marriage—to find success as a writer and a person. I found a woman who turned those early difficulties to her advantage, who grew stronger in the face of adversity.

Above all, I found that Marjory Stoneman Douglas was a woman of integrity. She was a woman of great courage who was willing, always, to speak her mind and to stand up for what she believed in, whether it was arguing against the builders who wanted to drain the Everglades in South Florida or speaking in favor of civil rights for African Americans at a time when the Ku Klux Klan still marched in the streets of Miami. She was an early feminist who worked for equality for women when they were considered second-class citizens. She was an opinionated woman who wasn't afraid to make her opinions known—whether she was talking about Ernest Hemingway's writing style (she didn't like it) or practicing celibacy outside of marriage (she was all for it). All told, Marjory Stoneman Douglas was one of the most fascinating women of recent history.

Any writer or reader interested in Marjory Stoneman Douglas's life must, of needs, read *Voice of the River*, her autobiography, written with Miami journalist John Rothchild. This book provides basic information about Douglas's life and insights into her thoughts that can be found in no other source. Without it on my desk, I would have been stymied.

Unfortunately, there are—even with *Voice of the River* in hand—blank spots in Douglas's life, areas in which a biographer is forced to surmise about her thoughts and feelings. I've tried to keep this guesswork to a minimum. Where I've been forced to speculate, I used my own common sense and knowledge about Douglas to make the best guess possible. And, of course, I've clearly indicated in the text when my words are conjecture rather than known, provable facts.

This book could not have been written without the help of many people. I want to particularly thank Craig Likness, Christine Layton, and Ruthanne Vogel, all members of the staff of the Otto G. Richter Library at the University of Miami, in Miami, Florida; and Maria McNally, librarian of the Taunton High School Library in Taunton, Massachusetts. Of course, I want to thank my wife, Lynne, who provided her usual moral support and copyediting skills.

Chapter One

The Beginning

The crowd in the high school auditorium
in South Florida was in a nasty mood.
Landowners and property developers who
wanted to drain a swath of the Everglades not
far from Miami hissed and booed as a tiny
woman, a floppy straw hat perched on her
white hair, a strand of pearls around her neck,
shuffled slowly to a microphone at the
front of the room.
"Go back to Russia, Grandma!" one of the men
in the sweltering hot room roared.
"Go home, you Commie!" another shouted.[1]

But Marjory Stoneman Douglas was not about to be silenced on that day almost thirty years ago. Having come to the auditorium to protect the Everglades from developers, she was determined to speak her piece. And when she was determined, she was a fighter. Though she looked frail, she was, in her own words, "about as frail as a small, coarse horse."[2]

As boos and catcalls washed over her, she stared out at the audience through eyeglass lenses thick as bottle bottoms. Only about five feet tall and weighing about one hundred pounds, she stood stoically until the crowd grew quiet. "That's all right," she said, her voice strong and vibrant. "Carry on. I'm an old lady, and I can take the heat. I can stay here all night."[3] Then she began speaking—"elocuting," she called it—against the developers' plans.

On that occasion, Marjory Stoneman Douglas was successful. A friend who listened to her talk remembered years later, "She said her piece with eloquence and humor and a bit of snap. When the evening was over, the Everglades in that area (was protected)."[4]

When she spoke at that hearing, Douglas—then in her eighties—was a world-famous author. About two decades earlier she had been asked by an editor to write a book about the Miami River. Not sure she could write a book of several hundred pages about a river that is only some thirty miles long, she asked the editor if he would be interested in a book about the region most Floridians call the 'Glades. The editor agreed and the result was her celebrated book, *The Everglades: River of Grass.*

Published in 1947, Douglas's book was a beautifully written mix of history and easily understood science that painted a striking picture of the importance of the Everglades. It was an instant success and transformed the way many people looked at the river of grass. As successful as it was, though, it did little to stop development of the region many people saw as nothing but a useless swamp. Over the years, drainage and development of the Everglades continued. Eventually Douglas and a small group of fellow conservationists formed an organization—Friends of the Everglades—to save the wetlands. She became the spokesperson for the group. She spoke to anybody who would listen about the importance of the region to Florida and to the world.

To Marjory Stoneman Douglas, protecting the Everglades was all important. "The Everglades must be taken care of," she once said. "There's a job to do and it must be done."[5] She did it so well that she is famous today as "The Voice of the Everglades."

If Marjory Stoneman Douglas had done no more than write her book and battle to preserve the Everglades, her life would have been remarkable. But there was much more to her life than her role as an author and environmentalist. Indeed, this woman who was born when Queen Victoria sat on the throne of England and Benjamin Harrison was president of the United States, who was alive when Halley's comet appeared in the night sky both in 1910 and again in 1986, lived a life filled with accomplishments despite the fact that she had to overcome early setbacks that might have crushed a woman of less courage and spirit.

Marjory Stoneman Douglas visits the Florida Everglades in 1989.

$\mathcal{M}$arjory Stoneman Douglas was born in Minneapolis, Minnesota, on April 7, 1890. Her father, Frank Stoneman, was the co-owner of a savings and loan association. Her mother, Florence Lillian Trefethen, was a musically talented women who might have had a career as a concert violinist if the opportunity had presented itself. Instead, like virtually all women in the late 1800s, Lillian, as she was always called, was a homemaker.

At the time of Marjory's birth, Minneapolis was a boom town. Surrounded by fertile farmland and thick forests, the city was one of the nation's leading flour- and lumber-producing centers.

Although Frank Stoneman was part owner of his company, the Stoneman family wasn't wealthy. They lived comfortably in a rented apartment in a Minneapolis boardinghouse. As an only child, Marjory was coddled and probably a bit spoiled. In those days fat babies were considered healthy babies. Marjory was, she said, "plied with the best of butter, cream, pancakes and everything fattening there was."[6] Much later in her life, she remembered sitting on a flight of stairs in that Minneapolis boardinghouse, being fed from a pan of warm creamed potatoes. It was, she said, the only memory she had of those days.

Unfortunately, this happy period at the beginning of Marjory's life did not last long. When she was three years old, Frank Stoneman lost his business. Frank, Lillian, and Marjory moved to Providence, Rhode Island, probably to be closer to Frank Stoneman's mother and other family members who lived there and who might help them financially.

Marjory at age one and a half

Marjory's mother, Lillian Stoneman, in a photograph probably taken just before she married Frank

During the next few years, Marjory's whole world fell apart. To be sure, there were some happy moments. Marjory remembered her mother playing the piano for visitors to their rented duplex apartment and fondly recalled her father holding her in his lap as he read to her. But most of Marjory's memories of her childhood were sad.

Frank Stoneman—more of a philosopher than a businessman—was unable to make any money. At the same time, Lillian Stoneman did not get along well with her in-laws who lived within shouting distance of the apartment the Stoneman's rented. The stresses of the family's financial situation and the constant bickering with her husband's relatives contributed to what Marjory later described as her mother's mental break-down—mental illness that would tragically color the rest of Lillian Stoneman's life.

One of Marjory's most vivid memories of those days was of a violent argument she saw between her mother and her cousin, Forrest Rundell. It was, she later said, one of the first hints she had that something terrible was happening to her mother. In the middle of that argument Lillian laughed in an eerie, terrifying, almost otherworldly way. "It was the first time I'd heard such a laugh," Marjory said almost ninety years later. "It frightened me so much that I can still hear it today."[7]

That was just the beginning, though. As time passed, Lillian Stoneman's mental illness grew worse. Eventually, taking five-year-old Marjory with her, she abandoned her husband, fleeing from the house in

Providence and running away to Taunton, Massachusetts, where her parents lived. Marjory was not to see her father again for many years.

In Taunton, Marjory and her mother lived in the Trefethen family home, a big, three-story, Victorian-style house. There, Lillian Stoneman's mental illness continued to worsen. She screamed at other members of the family for no apparent reason. She woke in the middle of the night to laugh and talk uncontrollably. Through it all, Marjory watched, confused and terrified, often seeking shelter in her grandfather's arms where she felt safe.

Lillian's parents did as much as they could to help their daughter. They hired a private nurse to watch over her. Eventually, however, she was hospitalized in a local sanitarium.

While Marjory later talked openly about that painful time in her life, she never wrote in detail about her feelings during those terrible and terrifying years, first in Providence and then later in Taunton. It's easy to imagine, though, what it must have been like for a five-year-old girl as she watched her parents' marriage disintegrate and her mother slipping deeper and deeper into insanity.

"There were," she said, "the bad dreams from which I often woke myself screaming." Sometimes, she later recalled, she would find herself half asleep, half awake, walking around her room in the middle of the night, her arms over her head, her hands flapping as if she were a bird trying to fly into the darkness. "It seemed as if there were some enormous thing by my left ear, some enormous thing that was going to explode with a loud noise at any moment."[8]

In the midst of all this turmoil, when Marjory was about six years old, she was enrolled in a grammar school within walking distance of her grandparents' home. In a way, school was a lifesaver for the little girl who was surrounded by fear and stress and pain in her grandparents' home. Even ninety years later she remembered the name of her first teacher, Florence Francis.

Marjory was a good student though, by her own admission, she was not good at arithmetic and did not understand fractions. "The teacher," she later said, "tried to demonstrate fractions by cutting up an apple." From that day forward, Marjory added, she "always hated apples as well as fractions. . . ."[9] Still, she did do well enough in school to skip the second grade.

At school, Marjory started to read voraciously. Soon, reading was her favorite activity, a way to escape from her problems. All she wanted was to lose herself in a good book until it was time for her to go to school once again.

Meanwhile, probably around the time that Marjory started school, her mother returned home. Though she was no longer as sick as she'd been, she was still not well. Perhaps because of medicine she was given to treat her illness, she was, Marjory said, childlike. She had a disturbing habit of doing little irresponsible things, often moving items from their accustomed place in the home for no reason, even though she knew it bothered others in her family. At the same time, Lillian had developed a strong dislike for her own mother and frequently quarreled with her and with Marjory's Aunt Fanny, who also lived in the family home.

In the years immediately following Lillian's return home, as Marjory continued going to school, she and her mother began isolating themselves from the others in the big Victorian house. Mother and daughter would stay downstairs, while Lillian's parents and sister and brother—perhaps to avoid having to witness the effects of Lillian's illness—spent most of their time upstairs. In these strange circumstances, Lillian Stoneman became both Marjory's best friend and her "child." They played children's games together and napped together when Marjory was home from school. In the evenings they often went for long walks together. When it was time for bed, they climbed the stairs to their rooms together.

And so Marjory passed her childhood. She went to school. She played with her mother and a few girl-friends she made at school. She found books—in her grandfather's library and at the town library—to read, to revel in, for comfort and escape. She read the works of Charles Dickens—volumes she found in her grandfather's library and still had in her home in Florida at the time of her death almost a full century later. She read *Swiss Family Robinson* and other adventure stories. And if there wasn't anything else to read, she read the encyclopedia. Marjory once said that the trauma of her young life made her a person with an "active and hidden inner life, secretive and imaginative, based on reading and daydreaming."[10]

Marjory's lack of friends and her withdrawal into the solitude of books was surely related to her unstable home life but may also have been because of how she felt about herself. She described herself as homely, nothing like her mother, who was a very pretty woman, or, for that matter, her father, who was equally good-looking in a rakish kind of way. Chubby, with what she said was stringy mouse-colored hair, Marjory wore gold-rimmed glasses she called the "crowning unattractive feature on an unattractive child."[11]

In reality, Marjory's assessment of her looks was much too harsh. Still, it is obvious that Marjory certainly felt unattractive. That could only have added to her pain and sadness.

It seems very unlikely that any who knew Marjory as her childhood came to an end and she prepared to begin high school could have imagined what lay in store for her. It seems certain that none who knew her in Taunton could have even guessed that this sad, chubby, introverted girl, forced by circumstances to be a parent to her own mother, finding her greatest pleasure in books, would ultimately find worldwide fame as an author, an early fighter for civil rights, and an environmental activist.

Chapter Two

Coming of Age

In 1904, when she was fourteen years of age, Marjory Stoneman started the ninth grade at a high school not far from her grandparents' house in Taunton. While Marjory later said her life at that time looked normal and happy to outsiders, her life was anything but pleasant. The situation at her grandparents' home was still depressing. In fact, her life inside that house was so troubled that many years later Marjory's memories of that time still filled her with sadness.

Often, people who are in pain use humor as a way to protect themselves, to hide feelings that may be too painful to face head on. In the *Taunton High School Journal and Stylus* of 1908, a combination yearbook and literary magazine, Marjory wrote this clearheaded assessment of herself: "I have always more need of a laugh than a cry, being somewhat disposed to melancholy in my temperament."[1] Apparently, Marjory's attempts to escape the pain of her home life through humor worked well. Her classmates at Taunton High School described her as "giggling . . . with a sense of humor."[2]

As a very young girl, Marjory's world had been limited to her grandparent's house, school, and the public library where she was able to escape for brief periods. As a high-school student growing into young womanhood, her horizons expanded. She had girlfriends with whom she shared adventures and, no doubt, secrets and hopes and dreams. She went camping in New Hampshire with Margaret Blaine, one of those friends. She read and discussed books with her friend Edith Siebel. After her uncle Charlie taught her how to sail a small boat, she went sailing at the lake near Taunton with Madeline Beers, another of her friends.

Naturally enough, Marjory became interested in boys during her high-school years. But while her girlfriends were asked to parties and cotillions by boys they knew in school, Marjory wasn't. She went to dances, but was rarely asked to dance. "That's when I began to experience the awful ordeal of being a wallflower," she later said.[3] In fact, she still thought of herself as a fat, rather ugly girl. Little wonder, then, that she was terribly self-conscious around boys and had a tendency to giggle because of her nervousness.

While boys did not pay attention to her, Marjory was very popular with her girlfriends. Probably as a way to compensate for her disappointment at being a wall-flower, she arranged parties and games she could play with her friends. Sometimes eight or ten girls would get together and play tag or kick the can, hard exercise in those days when girls wore long skirts and heavy jackets and hats even when they were playing outdoors.

Marjory became so well known as a party organizer that the same edition of the *Journal and Stylus* that described her as "giggling" also included a teasing reference to her ability as a party- and game-planner. A make-believe classified advertisement in that publication offered the services of "Miss Marjory Stoneman" as a "Wholesale Dealer in Ideas for Parties, Club Meetings, and Social Gatherings of all kinds." The ad went on to offer "special prices for ideas by the dozens or the hundred."[4]

During her years at Taunton High School, Marjory began to write seriously. Just before her graduation, a short sketch she wrote—"Waiting for a Train"—was published in the *Journal and Stylus*. By that time, Marjory had been accepted as a student at Wellesley College, the famous women's school not far from Boston. She may have thought of her idea for "Waiting for a Train" as she stood at the railroad station in Taunton, her suitcase by her side, waiting for a commuter train that would carry her to Boston, where she boarded a trolley bound for the small town of Wellesley and the college.

Only about a half page in length, "Waiting for a Train" shows that as a teenager Marjory was an accomplished observer of people and events around her. Her work also showed that she had a writer's ability to record what she saw in a lively way.

When Marjory left home to become a student at Wellesley, an exciting new world opened to her. For the first time in her life she was on her own.

Naturally enough, Marjory had mixed feelings about leaving home. She later said she felt a "terrible sorrow" at having to abandon her mother. But it was sorrow that was mixed with a sense of freedom. "It was as if some of the burden I'd carried since I was six years old was lifted," Marjory said. "There was a new joy in life, in living, and in experience."[5]

Founded in 1870, Wellesley College is located on a wooded campus on the banks of Lake Waban about 13 miles from Boston. In her first letter home, Marjory wrote glowingly of the scarlet leaves of the trees that dotted the campus and how those leaves were mirrored in the still waters of the lake. While she didn't mention it in her letter, she must also have been struck by the classic beauty of College Hall, a four-story gothic structure with soaring spires overlooking Lake Waban. At that time the hall was the college's only building.

When Marjory became a Wellesley student, the college had no living quarters for its first-year students.

The gym at Wellesley in the early 1900s.

Freshmen lived in the village of Wellesley itself. Marjory took a room in a boardinghouse—the cheapest room in the house, in the attic. Though the room was cramped, she loved it with its blue-and-white wallpaper and a tiny window under the eaves looking out over a garden and trees.

Like many college freshmen, Marjory had no idea what work she wanted to do when she finished her education. Her grandmother, who was paying for her schooling with help from Marjory's Aunt Fanny, wanted her to become a teacher—one of just a handful of careers open to educated women in 1908. Marjory, however, had no desire to spend her workdays in a classroom. In fact, she said she hated the idea. Uncertain of her plans, she decided to major in English composition.

As it had been in high school, composition was Marjory's favorite class. The English department at Wellesley was a "great" department, she later said.[6] Its faculty included several published writers including Katharine Lee Bates, who wrote the words to "America the Beautiful," the Wellesley College song that became almost as famous as the "Star-Spangled Banner." With the guidance of these teachers, Marjory spread her creative wings and soon gained a reputation among her classmates as a gifted writer.

Of course, there was more to college than just writing. Like all students, Marjory took science and mathematics and geography and a required Bible course that was, according to Marjory, more like a literature course than a course in religion.

Marjory particularly enjoyed public-speaking classes where she learned how to speak clearly and to project her voice so that she could be heard even in the back of a large room. Later in her life, when she began speaking out about protecting Florida's Everglades, these skills proved to be invaluable. "I studied elocution at Wellesley College," she often said, "and I've been going around elocuting ever since."[7]

If composition and elocution were her favorite classes, "gymnasium," or physical education, was her least favorite. An old photo of the Wellesley gymnasium taken about the time that Marjory was a freshman shows a group of students dressed in long dark dresses and dark stockings climbing ropes attached to overhead beams while other girls do floor exercises. Marjory hated the exercises so much that she lied to her teachers, telling them that she had rheumatism that made climbing ropes and doing push-ups too painful to endure.

Though she was excused from gymnasium class, Marjory was still required to find a form of exercise she could do comfortably. She decided to—in her words—"whack around at a golf ball" on a little golf course not far from the college campus. "It was lovely walking out in the country air," she said.[8] Indeed, she found it so lovely that she wrote an essay called "Lost Balls" about how tracking down lost golf balls was a perfect excuse for taking a walk in the country. That essay was published in the college literary magazine.

Another essay of Marjory's published in 1908 was about a Wellesley tradition known as "Tree Day." On that

Marjory chose golf as a replacement for the required
gym class at Wellesley. This picture shows
Wellesley golfers around 1904.

day in May each year, the students marched together in costumes to a spot on campus where one of the freshmen planted a small tree or two. After the trees were planted, poems were recited, the students danced around a maypole or staged elaborate skits, and a song was sung by the gathered students in front of College Hall.

Marjory took part in the Tree Day ceremony of 1910 when all the students united in presenting "A Merrie Festival performed before her Majestie, Queene Elizabeth of England." Unfortunately we don't know what part Marjory played, or her reaction to the pomp and circumstance surrounding a visit from the queen.

Marjory also must have taken part in other Wellesley traditions including what one student called a "secret and very strange" ceremony. This ritual, performed by senior students at sunrise on May 1 each year, involved thoroughly scrubbing a huge marble statue of a woodsman that stood on the porch of College Hall overlooking the lake. As they worked, the senior students sang:

> *"We are the Seniors*
> *Seniors are we*
> *Washing the Woodsman*
> *Right Merrily."*[9]

For Marjory, still shy around young men, still, in her own mind, unattractive and underdeveloped, Wellesley was a perfect environment. Even much later in her life, she wrote with obvious affection for the college. "Wellesley has always been one of the great influences in my life," she said, "and in our day it was especially important as a college for women, where they could find out more about themselves and their abilities without being distracted by the boys."[10]

Meanwhile, though Marjory enjoyed the companionship of her female friends and classmates, there were times when she was lonely. She had no dates at all during the four years she was in college. Secretly, she said, she was "immensely attracted" to young men, and "suffered a great deal" when these young men didn't pay attention to her.[11]

Her loneliness aside, Wellesley was a positive experience for Marjory. After she got a room of her own in College Hall in her junior year, she began to flower as a writer. She also grew more confident in her own abilities. It was at Wellesley that she began to see that women have the right to put their skills—whatever they are—to use in the world and not to depend on men for happiness. In line with these beliefs, Marjory became a suffragette during her college years, joining with a small number of her classmates in working to give women the right to vote.

Hanging over her during these years was the dark cloud of Lillian Stoneman's madness and the guilt Marjory felt about leaving her still-sick mother in Taunton. In her junior year, that guilt must have grown almost unbearable when she learned that her mother had breast cancer. In the spring and summer between her junior and senior years, Marjory spent as much time as she could at home, taking time out only to work briefly as a counselor at a girl's camp in Maine.

Marjory's portrait for the
1912 Wellesley yearbook

By the end of the summer, her mother seemed to be recovering, and Marjory returned to Wellesley. Soon, she was swept up in the excitement of school. As a senior, she had a scholarship that enabled her to get a private room with a balcony in College Hall, overlooking Lake Waban. She excelled in her classes and was named the editor of the college annual. She acted in the senior play and was elected Class Orator.

Commencement Day, she later remembered, was lovely, marked by processions and parades and special events. Her Aunt Fanny and a cousin were in the audience as she received her degree.

After the ceremonies ended, her aunt delivered terrible news from the home in Taunton, news she hadn't wanted to share until Marjory had graduated. Her mother's cancer had metastasized, or spread. She was dying, slipping in and out of a coma, her waking moments periods of terrible pain. Marjory rushed home, just in time to spend a few days with her mother before she died.

Her mother's death must have been something of a relief for Marjory who had spent days sitting by the dying woman's bedside, watching her suffer. At the same time, her mother's death meant there was no reason for Marjory to remain in Taunton. With a college degree, she was ready to strike out on her own.

No doubt, Marjory felt excited at the prospect of beginning a new phase of life. Fortunately for her, she had no idea what grief and confusion and loneliness lay ahead.

Chapter Three

Into the World

In the summer of 1912, following graduation from college and the death of her mother, twenty-one-year-old Marjory Stoneman moved to Boston. There, using money borrowed from a college friend, she rented a tiny apartment.

Though she had a degree in English, Marjory was uncertain about what she wanted to do with her life. Unlike many women at that time, Marjory was not ready to get married as soon as she finished school. In any case, she had no marriage prospects. That meant she needed a job.

That summer was a difficult time for Marjory. She later said she felt numb with grief. She had a sense of being disconnected from her surroundings as she tried to begin her life as a career woman. Nevertheless, with an eye to finding work, she enrolled in a course that would help her find employment supervising sales clerks in department stores. Somehow, she managed to complete the training course in Boston.

In the fall, soon after completing her training, Marjory learned that her closest college friend, Carolyn Percy, had found a job as a teacher at a private school in St. Louis, Missouri, and had room for her in her apartment at the school. By the time the weather turned cold, Marjory had obtained work at Nugent's Department Store in St. Louis. For $15 a week, she was placed in charge of the store's sales clerks.

While $15 today would barely pay for a large pizza, it was a fairly substantial amount of money in 1912, enough to pay Marjory's room and board with a little extra to buy some new clothing. She made some changes in her appearance. She lost weight and took pains to make herself more attractive. Those external changes, however, did little to make Marjory feel better about herself. "I felt like a misfit, a misfit with a job," she later said.[1]

What was an unhappy situation became even less happy when her friend Carolyn left St. Louis to return to her family home in New York. In the fall of 1913, not long after Carolyn's departure, Marjory moved yet again. This time she relocated to Newark, New Jersey, where she found employment as educational director at a department store. Her job was to teach basic skills including mathematics and grammar to salesgirls. For this she was paid $20 a week.

In Newark, Marjory rented a tiny apartment near the department store where she worked, just across the street from one of the city's public libraries. Living alone, she was, she later said, very lonely. "It wasn't life, it was just making a living."[2]

Little did Marjory know as she went to work each day and visited the public library, that her loneliness and the emptiness of her life made her vulnerable. Despite her obvious intelligence, she had no way of realizing that this vulnerability would lead her to make a decision that would ultimately fill her life with turmoil and pain.

What was to be a terribly difficult period of her life began innocently and happily enough one afternoon on the sidewalk outside the department store where Marjory worked. At that time she was introduced to Kenneth Douglas. A reporter for the *Newark Evening News* newspaper, Douglas was, Marjory said, a "tall, thin and intelligent-looking man."[3]

A few weeks after that first encounter, Marjory and Douglas had what she later described as "a fateful meeting" near the main desk of the local library. After chatting for a few moments, Marjory was amazed to see that Douglas was looking at her with what she described as "intense personal interest."[4]

Marjory Stoneman, the perennial wallflower who thought of herself as overweight and plain, the lonely young woman who was never asked to dance, was flabbergasted by the tall, handsome reporter's attentions.

Over the next several weeks, Kenneth relentlessly courted her. He called her on the phone, visited her in the store, took her to lunch, and out on dates. She was overwhelmed, swept off her feet.

Just a few weeks after their meeting in the library, Douglas asked Marjory to marry him. Though a small inner voice told her that she was making a mistake, she waited only about five minutes before telling him she would be his wife.

Indeed, agreeing to marry the smooth-talking, Ireland-born reporter was a mistake, a terrible mistake. By her own admission, Marjory knew almost nothing about Kenneth Douglas except that he was good-looking, had charming manners, and that he told her he loved her. Still, on April 18, 1914, about three months after their first meeting, they were married in a small ceremony in Newark.

Though it would take Marjory several years and a great deal of pain, she later came to believe that in Kenneth Douglas she had found a father figure to replace the man who had abandoned her as a child. Douglas was, after all, tall and slender like her father. It also seems that Marjory thought of Douglas as being much older than she was. Late in her life, she described Douglas as being about thirty years older than she was. The certificate of their marriage, however, shows that at the time of the marriage he was thirty-four, just ten years older than she.[5]

There's no doubt that even as she took her vows, Marjory was unsure about what she was doing. She did not even tell her family she was engaged and kept her marriage secret from her aunt and grandmother and most of her friends until after she was Mrs. Kenneth Douglas. "I simply had no power of judgment over anything," she later said.[6]

Immediately following the ceremony, the couple traveled by train to New York City. There, they enjoyed a brief honeymoon.

According to Marjory, her introduction to married life—or at least the sexual side of marriage—was nothing short of wonderful.

Like most young women in the early 1900s, Marjory knew virtually nothing about sex before her marriage. Even in what were known as sex hygiene classes she attended at Wellesley, she later said, real sex education was lacking. "Nothing was said whatsoever about how you got pregnant, except that it was a secret process," she added.[7]

As a consequence of her ignorance about sex, Marjory came to her marriage bed filled with curiosity. That curiosity quickly changed to gusto as she discovered that she was a passionate woman who thoroughly enjoyed sex.

After their honeymoon, Marjory and Kenneth Douglas returned to Newark. There she belatedly introduced her new husband to her aunts and other members of her family. Like Marjory, they were charmed by the suave newspaperman's good looks and good manners.

In Newark, the newlyweds found a two-room apartment with a small kitchenette and bath. The kitchen was so small that dishes and cooking utensils had to be stored on a sideboard in the sitting room. Kenneth went to work each day at the *Newark Evening News*. Marjory quit her job and stayed home, preparing meals and washing and ironing and cleaning for her husband.

For a brief time Marjory was happy in her role as a housewife. She became a proper homemaker, content to care for her husband, volunteering to read to the blind in her spare time.

Sadly, that period of happiness didn't last very long. Kenneth Douglas, it turned out, was an alcoholic and a petty crook. Within a few months of their honeymoon, he was arrested for writing a worthless check.

Blinded by what she thought was love or perhaps by her need for this father figure in her life, Marjory stood by her husband. For six months, while he was in a New Jersey prison, she visited him each weekend. Upon his release, when he moved to New York to get a fresh start, she went to join him, even though her family wanted her to end the marriage.

The months that followed Marjory's reunion with her husband in early 1915 were what she described as "some odd times."[8] Unable to find regular work, the couple lived from hand-to-mouth, often in hotels not much better than skid-row tenements, sometimes forced to flee in the middle of the night to avoid bill collectors.

In those months Marjory did not even bother looking for work. She spent hours sitting in rented rooms, reading. She felt, she later said, as if she was in a state of suspended animation. It was if she'd turned her will over to her husband and blindly followed wherever he led.

Though Marjory did not know it, her husband was drinking heavily outside the home during this period. He was also involved in petty crime again. She must have been terrified when he left her alone for days at a time. Still, her dependency on her sick husband—or her need for his love—was so strong that she tolerated his behavior.

Marjory's strange, directionless life grew downright bizarre in the spring of 1915 when Kenneth somehow got in touch with her father, the man she had not seen for two decades. While Marjory later said she was unsure just what Kenneth had in mind, it seems he tried to forge bank drafts using Frank Stoneman's name. While that plan failed, it alerted Marjory's father that his daughter was in trouble . . . a great deal of trouble.

Justifiably worried, Frank Stoneman quickly got in touch with his brother, a physician who lived in Springfield, Massachusetts. Within a few days, Marjory's Uncle Ned came to Newark and found his niece.

Perhaps Marjory, like many women of that era, felt she needed a man to lead her. Maybe she simply needed somebody outside her marriage to force her to take a cold, hard look at her situation. Or perhaps she only needed someone—anyone—to offer her a way out of a situation that had become intolerable.

In any event, Marjory's uncle told her that she had to get away from Kenneth Douglas or that her whole life would be ruined. He also let her know that her father, living in Florida, had recently gotten married for the second time. He told her that Frank Stoneman and his new wife both wanted Marjory to come live with them, at least for a few months.

As her uncle talked to her, Marjory knew he was right. "I knew I couldn't go on the way I'd been living," she said.[9] Immediately, she decided she would leave her husband, move to Florida to live with her father, and obtain a divorce from Kenneth Douglas.

The end of the marriage was quick. Soon after her talk with her uncle, Marjory told her husband she was leaving him for good. That same night she and Kenneth walked together to a nearby trolley stop. They sat together for a time on a stone wall, talking softly. As Kenneth boarded the trolley, Marjory said good-bye and walked away, never to see her husband again.

Like many divorced women in her time, Marjory decided to keep her husband's name even after her marriage ended. In her autobiography, written when she was almost ninety years of age, Marjory said she felt no regret either over her marriage or about leaving it. It was "an education."[10]

However, it is possible to gain at least a bit more insight into how Marjory felt about the end of her marriage in "Pineland," a short story she wrote about a decade after she and Kenneth broke up. The main character in that story—a woman named Sarah McDevitt—is trapped in a bad marriage. In one passage, the woman admits she had married a man who was unsuitable because she had been afraid of being alone. "I guess that's why I married him when he came along when ma died . . . ," Douglas had written.

In another passage in that same story, Sarah McDevitt spoke of how she felt when her husband left her. "He would have liked me to beg him to [stay]," Douglas wrote. "I never let on that my knees were like string to see him go. He turned at the gate and smiled at me over that orange-colored beard with his stone white teeth and his eyes that were like wires boring into you, and I shut my mouth tight and let him look. So he stopped smiling and went. . . ."[11]

Despite Douglas's claim that she felt only relief to be free from Kenneth Douglas, that passage gives us a hint that she might, in reality, have felt a real sense of loss when her marriage—like that of the character in her story—ended. At the very least, it must have been painful for her to realize that she had made a terrible mistake. It would have been perfectly natural for her to question her own judgment, to wonder how she could have put herself at the mercy of an alcoholic and petty thief.

Douglas's strange, painful marriage proved to be a defining moment in her life. It convinced her, she later said, of the foolishness of allowing herself to be dominated by another person—particularly by a man. Her marriage made her value her independence—the independence that was at the core of her later life as a writer, social activist, and environmentalist. In that sense, it was a blessing.

Though Douglas could not have known it at the time, her decision in mid-1915 to move to Florida and to live with her father—by that time a newspaper editor in Miami—was to change her life in ways she could never have imagined. This decision proved to be the first step along a meandering path that would ultimately gain Marjory Stoneman Douglas lasting, worldwide fame.

Chapter Four

A New Beginning

In September 1915, twenty-five-year-old Marjory Stoneman Douglas traveled by train from Newark, New Jersey, to New York City. There she boarded another train bound for Florida and a reunion with the father she had not seen in twenty years.

As the train made its way out of Grand Central Station and headed south, Douglas was filled with a sense of freedom and excitement. At the same time, she must have been apprehensive. After all, she was turning her back on the life she had known for years, about to meet a man she barely remembered.

Douglas had plenty of time to think as the train made its slow way from New York through Philadelphia and then into Virginia, the Carolinas, and Georgia. No doubt she wondered what lay ahead for her, what would become of her, what kind of welcome she'd get from Frank Stoneman and his new wife.

After about thirty-six hours of travel, the train crossed the border between Georgia and Florida not far from Jacksonville. Douglas was not, at first, impressed by the sight of the state that would be her home for the next eighty-three years. In fact, she described the three-hundred-mile train ride from Jacksonville to Miami, where her father lived, as "interminable." There was nothing to look at, she said, but "pine trees for hour after hour, an infinity of pine trees."[1]

Later in her life, Douglas developed a passionate love for the land and the landscape she first saw outside her train window in 1915. In "Pineland," the short story she wrote in 1925, she described Florida's pines with obvious affection: "They were strange trees, strange but beautiful . . . ," she wrote. "They were endlessly alike, endlessly monotonous, and yet with an endless charm and variety."[2]

Finally, at 7:00 A.M., the train arrived in Miami. Douglas was sleeping in a Pullman compartment when the train pulled into the small white-and-yellow train depot in the middle of what is now downtown Miami. She rose, hurriedly dressed, and stepped off the train. Her father was to meet her at 9:00 A.M., so she knew she had time to go sightseeing. Wanting to see the bay that borders Miami, she headed east in the early morning sunshine.

Douglas had bought a new blue serge dress for her trip south. Her outfit was ideal for a northern September day, but quickly proved to be uncomfortable in South Florida's warm weather. "I was hot and sticky," she said, "but I liked the heat."[3]

Though she enjoyed the warmth as she walked east from the train station, she was not impressed by the town of Miami. It was, in her eyes, ugly and uninteresting, a collection of small wooden buildings along with a few boardinghouses, interspersed with trees that looked strange, nothing like the trees she was used to up north. As she walked along she had to squint her eyes against the blinding glare of the sun as it reflected streets paved with white limestone. Then, suddenly, the vista opened up and she was standing on the edge of Biscayne Bay, an expanse of water that stretches between Miami and the offshore island known as Miami Beach.

"It was cool, blue and green, with the wind coming off the sea in the slanting early morning sunlight," she later said. The bay, she added, "was a wonderful setting at the edge of a second-rate town."[4]

The Miami that Douglas found in 1915 was nothing like the vibrant metropolis of today. For most of the nearly five centuries since Juan Ponce de León first sailed into the waters of South Florida in 1513, only a handful of hardy souls even attempted to live permanently in the inhospitable, isolated region around Miami. It wasn't until the mid-1800s that the region began to see any serious attempt at settlement. At that time, homesteaders, hardy men and women who barely

Flagler Street in Miami around the time that
Douglas first arrived in Florida

49 /

managed to eke out a hardscrabble existence in one of the world's least friendly environments, started moving into the region. They were followed by a few shopkeepers and saloonkeepers and other hangers-on but still, as late as 1895, it seemed that Miami was destined to be no more than a backwoods village.

That began to change in 1896. At that time, Henry Flagler, a wealthy railroad magnate, completed a rail line from Jacksonville to Miami. The next year he built the luxurious 350-room Royal Palm Hotel on the north shore of the Miami River, in what is now downtown Miami. Where the railroads went, people followed. By the time Douglas stepped off the train in Miami, the city had a population of about five thousand people.

Of course, on that September morning in 1915, Douglas was more concerned about her own future than she was about Miami's past. By 9:00 A.M., she was back on the train, waiting nervously for her father to arrive.

That meeting between Douglas and her father was uncomfortable for them both. According to Douglas, when tall, broad-shouldered Frank Stoneman saw her, he was obviously shocked by her appearance. He remembered her as a little girl with curly hair. Now, she said, her hair was "droopy" and her face, always somewhat crooked was, if anything, more crooked than before. Frank Stoneman quickly recovered himself.

"Hello, sweetheart," he said.

"Hello, Father," Douglas answered.[5]

And then he kissed her.

If Frank Stoneman was put off by his daughter's appearance he soon made up for it. His courtly behavior and his easygoing manner soon had Douglas at her ease. Within minutes, father and daughter were riding in a rented car across a bridge over the Miami River to her father's comfortable house in Riverside, one of Miami's first subdivisions. There she met her stepmother, Lillius. A woman who would be, Douglas said, her "first and best friend all my life in Florida."[6]

During the next several days, as Douglas settled into her room on the second floor of the house overlooking the river, she and her father and her new stepmother got to know each other. Lillius Stoneman—a great-great-grandaughter of Thomas Jefferson—opened her house to the young woman she'd never seen before and made her feel welcome.

Of course, Douglas and her father had a lot of catching up to do. During conversations in the airy home's living room or at a huge dining table that had once been owned by Jefferson, Douglas learned that Frank Stoneman had studied law after his marriage to Douglas's mother ended. Not long after he finished his studies, he moved to Florida where he settled in Orlando and established himself as an attorney. It was there that he met Lillius. Though the two had quickly fallen in love, they had not married until after Lillian Stoneman, Douglas's mother, had died.

Frank Stoneman, who had been an unsuccessful businessman when Douglas was a child, was no more successful as a lawyer in Florida. His fortunes changed, however, when he was given an old, flatbed printing press in payment of an outstanding debt. He loaded the press on a railcar and hauled it to Miami where he estab-

Marjory Stoneman Douglas's father,
Frank Stoneman

lished the city's first morning newspaper—a paper that is still being published today as the *Miami Herald.*

As the newspaper's publisher and editor, Stoneman became a community leader and gained the respect of his fellow Miamians, who called him "Judge" because of his legal training. Isadore Cohen, an early Miami settler, described him this way in his memoirs:

> Frank B. Stoneman, editor-in-chief of the *Miami Herald,* is noted for his valuable contribution to the progress of this community. . . . His just and liberal attitude on local, state and national issues evoked favorable comments from all classes of Miami's citizenship. His unfailing defense of the oppressed and his persistence and forceful advocacy of needed reforms have made him a host of friends and admirers all over the state.[7]

While Douglas made only veiled references to feelings toward her father, it is obvious that she was not immediately as big a fan of Frank Stoneman as were her fellow Miamians. It was natural, though, for her to feel some bitterness toward her father. After all, he had made no attempt to visit her while she was growing up and never sent money to support her or her mother. Frank Stoneman, meanwhile, justified his absence from Douglas's life, and the fact that he had not supported either his daughter or her mother, by saying that he was the one who had been abandoned.

Reading Douglas's autobiography, it is easy to picture Frank Stoneman as a rather cold and unfeeling man, at least when it came to his daughter. Even with Douglas back in his life in 1915, he acted disinterested in her early life, so disinterested that Douglas called this his one "blind spot."[8] Still, the father and daughter soon grew if not close, at least comfortable with each other. In what was then a backwoods town, without a library, they shared books and conversations and many interests.

Not long after Douglas's arrival in Miami, the *Miami Herald's* society editor was called out of town because of a family illness. At her father's urging, Douglas took her place. As soon as she started working as a professional journalist, she knew she'd found her calling.

"It was as if everything else that I had been doing since college had been all wrong and suddenly I found what I was meant to do," she later said. "I didn't care what I was writing about as long as it was writing."[9]

Soon, Douglas went from being a temporary employee, filling in for the absent society editor, to working full time. She wrote society columns and articles about happenings in Miami.

In the course of her work, she learned more and more about the city that had become her home. She discovered that the Royal Palm Hotel had been built on the site of an ancient Tequesta Indian burial mound and that developers working for Henry Flagler had destroyed the mound, scattering ancient remains, to build the hotel. She also learned that Flagler crews had used dynamite to open the mouth of the Miami River to ship traffic, and in the process caused Biscayne Bay to fill with silt and muck.

At the same time, she learned from her father of what he viewed as wrong-headed plans and efforts to drain the Everglades, the huge wetlands that lay to the west of Miami. At this early point in her writing career, Douglas did not write about environmental issues. It is almost certain, though, that the dismay she felt when she learned about the lost burial mound, the damage done to the bay, and the plans to drain the Everglades was the beginning of Douglas's interest in preserving the environment and protecting history, an interest that would come to full flower many years later.

In addition to making her aware of environmental issues, her position on the newspaper gave her a chance to rub elbows with some famous and powerful people. One of the notables she met was Clarence Darrow, the famous defense attorney. She also met William Jennings Bryan, a three-time presidential nominee who would, a decade later, face Darrow in a notable trial in which Tennessee schoolteacher John Scopes was charged with teaching Darwin's theory of evolution in violation of Tennessee law.

In the spring of 1916, just a few months after her arrival in Florida, Douglas—who had been a suffragette while she was at Wellesley—traveled with several other women to the Florida capitol in Tallahassee. There, the women urged lawmakers to pass the Nineteenth Amendment to the U.S. Constitution, the amendment giving women the right to vote. On that train trip, Douglas was joined by Mary Bryan, William Jennings Bryan's wife, and three other politically active women. All five of the women spoke to lawmakers.

"Well, the committee of the House is a large room with men sitting all around the edge of it, with a high brass spittoon between every two men," Douglas said years later. "And we did our best. I had my best hat and my best dress and everything, and everybody talked as intelligently as you possibly could. . . . It was like talking to the wall. . . . And Mrs. William Jennings Bryan made a marvelous speech, one of the best speeches I'd ever heard, about suffrage. So, of course, the House turned it down."[10]

During the summer of 1916, Douglas was a regular visitor to Miami Beach, then a largely undeveloped barrier island about two miles off the mainland coast. She and some friends rented one of the few cottages on the beach. They spent their free time swimming, enjoying cookouts on the sand, and sitting in the moonlight on a ridge overlooking the Atlantic Ocean, surrounded by sea lavender and the sound of the waves as they swept ashore.

During this period, Douglas fell in love again, this time with a young reporter from a rival Miami newspaper, the *Metropolis*. Douglas and her fellow journalist— she identified him only as "Andy"—grew close enough to discuss marriage. In 1916, however, World War I was already raging in Europe. Andy was drawn to the action even before the United States was formally involved in the war. He volunteered for service as an ambulance driver, was sent to France, and eventually joined the Lafayette Escadrille, a squadron of American aviators who served with the French Air Force.

In 1917, not long after Andy's departure for Europe, Douglas was sent by her father to write about a U.S. Navy ship that visited Miami to enlist men and women into the Naval Reserve. Her job was to interview a local woman who was about to become the first Florida woman to enlist. Something about the United States Navy attracted Douglas immediately. Perhaps she believed that by enlisting she would have a chance to get to France where she could see Andy again. In any event, she later said, before she knew what was happening she enlisted in the U.S. Navy.

Later, she phoned her father at his newspaper office. "Father," she said, "I've just joined the Navy. What's going to happen to the *Herald*?" Her father's answer was immediate. "What I'm wondering," he said, "is what's going to happen to the Navy?"[11]

Frank Stoneman was right to wonder. By her own admission, Douglas may have been the worst sailor ever to enlist. Having joined the navy on no more than a thoughtless whim, she soon found herself hating the routine of being in uniform, taking orders, and obeying rules. Her time in the navy, she said, was "the worst year of my life."[12]

Though she doesn't say so herself, her time in the U.S. Navy surely was made more miserable because she missed Andy and worried what might happen to him as a pilot. As she struggled in her job typing letters for navy brass in Miami, she became enthralled with the idea of going to Europe herself. In early 1918 she convinced the U.S. Navy to give her an official and honorable discharge. As soon as her discharge came through, she joined the American Red Cross as a volunteer and was immediately assigned to serve in France.

At the age of twenty-eight, Marjory Stoneman Douglas was about to experience a whole new world, a world only a tiny handful of American women of her generation could even imagine, let alone experience.

Chapter Five

Europe

As Douglas prepared to sail to England in the summer of 1918, World War I had been raging for four years. During those years, while a few men like Andy volunteered to fight with the British and Canadian military forces, the United States had remained out of the conflict as thousands upon thousands of European and Russian soldiers, sailors, and civilians died in what was then described as "the war to end all wars."

When America did formally enter the conflict in 1917, the nation's response was overwhelming.

Within a year, more than 300,000 American soldiers were in France. By the war's end, the total number of American soldiers sent to France reached about 2,000,000. At the same time, the American Red Cross sent almost 30,000 nurses and other volunteers to serve helping both soldiers and civilians in war-torn Europe.

When Douglas left the U.S. Navy to become one of the Red Cross volunteers known as Gray Ladies because of the color of the uniforms they wore, her primary motivation was, at least in part, to contribute to the war effort. While she hated the war and its devastation, she thought people who believed America should stay neutral were mistaken. The war was, in her eyes, a battle between right and wrong. "Pacifism isn't always noble," she said later in her life, "and isn't always intelligent." Then she added a phrase that could easily have served as her motto. "You have to stand up for some things in this world."[1]

At the same time, Douglas had her very personal reason for joining the Red Cross and accepting an immediate assignment to Paris. She knew Andy was in France, and her desire to see him was her greatest motivation, she said.

It's easy to imagine, then, how nervous Douglas was as she packed her bags for a voyage across the ocean, to a strange war-torn land, to see the young man she loved and hoped to marry.

Douglas's journey from Miami to Europe began with a train trip to New York where she was to board a ship bound for England. Arriving in New York with time to spare, she moved in with her college friend Carolyn Percy.

While the two young women became reacquainted and waited for Douglas's ship to sail, both became ill with the flu. According to Douglas, she and Carolyn recovered after about a month. While she doesn't say so herself, if they did indeed have influenza, they were fortunate to have survived. At that time the world was in the earliest stages of what would prove to be the infamous Spanish influenza pandemic (world-wide epidemic) of 1918.

While no one knows the origin of the flu, some medical historians believe the flu pandemic first appeared on March 11, 1918, when a soldier at Fort Riley, Kansas, complained of a fever, sore throat, and headache. Within a matter of hours, more than one hundred soldiers were sick. By the end of that week, that number had soared to five hundred. Many died within hours or days. According to one historian, "strapping recruits began the day in the pink and ended it drowning in their own secretions."[2]

Whatever the flu's origins, the illness soon swept through the cold, wet trenches of the war zone in Europe and eventually ravaged virtually every country on the globe. By the time it ran its course, an estimated 20 million people worldwide—more than 500,000 in the United States alone—were dead.

Though both Douglas and Carolyn were debilitated by their monthlong battle with the flu, they did recover. By September, Douglas was ready to join a group of Red

Cross women on board a ship about to sail from Quebec, Canada.

The passage to England took about a week. The weather was bad, as it often is in the North Atlantic in the fall and winter months. The ships in the convoy that included Douglas's were forced to sail blacked out, with no lights showing, because of the danger of attack by German submarines.

Douglas and those on the other vessels in the convoy knew they were like targets in a shooting gallery. All knew that America had been drawn into the war only after Germany declared "open season" on American ships, including unarmed merchant vessels like those carrying Douglas and the other Red Cross workers to Europe.

As Douglas's convoy made its way across the ocean, scores of hunter-killer U-boats patrolled the waters of the Atlantic searching for defenseless ships they could send to the bottom. Douglas must have been scared as her ship plunged through the dark water hour after hour. Still, she loved the ocean voyage, or at least she did once she got over an initial bout of seasickness and got her sea legs. "You've never seen the sea until you've seen it from a blacked-out ship," she later said. "I was so thrilled to walk the decks, I forgot all about how we were vulnerable to submarines."[3]

After what proved to be an uneventful crossing, Douglas and the other Red Cross workers arrived in England, and then quickly made their way to Paris.

Paris in the 1920s was every bit as beautiful
and exciting as it is today.

From her first moment in Paris, Douglas loved the city that has captured the hearts of millions of visitors. She loved its architecture, its parks and green spaces and its smoky blue sky. In her mind, it was an ideal city.

Her excitement at being in Paris, a city that only a fortunate few wealthy Americans of her generation could ever hope to visit, was heightened by the fact that she expected to see Andy at almost any moment. Almost as soon as she unpacked her bags she sent word to him—by that time he was a pilot assigned to an airfield not far from Paris—that she was in France.

As she waited for Andy to contact her, Douglas started her job writing press releases and dispatches for publications in America about the relief work the Red Cross was doing for children in France. One day, not long after her arrival, she was busy writing in an office at Red Cross headquarters in Paris when Andy walked in.

Even seventy years after that day, Douglas remembered seeing Andy for the first time in Paris as if the meeting had happened just a few moments earlier. He had been awarded the Croix de guerre—a French military decoration for bravery—and, Douglas said, he looked "wonderful in his uniform."[4]

While she and Andy were happy to see each other, Douglas soon realized that there was a "wall" between them that hadn't existed in Miami. Andy soon confessed that in the months of their separation he had had an affair with a young Frenchwoman.

For a woman who once said she was disgusted by the idea of extramarital sex, Douglas took the news of

Andy's affair with a great deal of grace. She knew, she said, that while she had been safe in Miami, he was facing death in aerial combat on an almost daily basis. Under those circumstances, she said, she understood what he had done. Just as important, from Douglas's point of view, Andy told her the affair was over and that he wanted to return to her.

While Douglas was able to face the news of his affair without tears, she did regret the news that he was returning almost immediately to the States. The war, in the fall of 1918, was coming to an end, he told her, adding that his tour of duty was ending and that he planned to return to Miami and find a job.

After Andy's departure, Douglas felt a sense of loneliness . . . the same loneliness that was such a large part of her early life. Her one consolation, she said, was the knowledge that Andy was waiting for her at home.

Still, as lonely as she was, Douglas found Paris an exciting place to be in the early 1900s. She loved it so much, she said, she was determined not to let her personal problems take away from her pleasure. She moved from the cramped room in the Red Cross headquarters building that had been her home since her arrival in Paris and rented a second-floor room in an inexpensive hotel. Though the room was bare it had a fireplace, a small sink where she could wash her hands and get water for tea, and a view of a garden.

Within a month of her arrival in Paris, rumors began circulating that the war was almost over just as Andy had predicted. The fall of 1918 was a time of intense

People poured out into the streets of Paris
to celebrate the end of World War I. It was
an event Douglas never forgot.

excitement in Paris. A war in which an estimated ten million people—including almost an entire generation of young Frenchmen, Englishmen, and Germans, along with thousands of Americans and Russians—lost their lives, was finally coming to end.

On November 11, when word spread through Paris that Germany had surrendered, a hush fell across Paris. Douglas was standing on a balcony looking down on the Rue de Rivoli when, suddenly, the silence of the city was shattered by the sound of the big guns that protected Paris as they roared, again and again, in celebration. As Douglas watched crowds move into the streets, hundreds of men and women and children laughing and crying at the same time, she felt that she was a witness to the remaking of the entire world. It was a moment she would never forget.

It was, indeed, a dramatic moment. In the minds of many people who had seen the war and its devastation, it was one of the most remarkable moments of their lives. Here's what a reporter for *The New York Times* wrote at the end of the war: "They stopped fighting at 11 o'clock this morning. In a twinkling, four years of killing and massacre stopped as if God had swept His omnipotent finger across the scene of world carnage and had cried 'Enough.'"[5]

Though the war was indeed over, and the carnage at an end, Douglas stayed in Paris and continued working. She wrote as many as five newspaper articles each day describing how Red Cross clinics were turned over to local authorities. In her work, she traveled throughout

France. Dressed in her bulky Red Cross uniform with its heavy ankle-length skirt and military-style jacket, she saw a France that was rarely seen by a typical tourist.

As the peace spread Douglas was sent farther afield. Some time in early 1919, she was dispatched to Italy where she visited Venice and Florence. Her next trip took her to the Balkans—present-day Croatia, Serbia, Montenegro, Albania, and Macedonia. She delivered medical supplies and food to refugees living in caves in Serbia and rode on horseback up and down craggy mountain paths in Albania. She saw sights she would remember for the rest of her life.

In her time in Europe, Douglas was particularly moved by the plight of refugee families who were in a state of shock after being uprooted by the war. Her experience in war-torn Europe helped her understand the needs of Latin American and Haitian refugees who came to Miami in search of freedom sixty years after the end of World War I.

By the fall of 1919, the Red Cross was ending its operations in Paris. At that time, Douglas's father sent her a telegram offering her a job as assistant editor of the *Miami Herald*. While part of Douglas wanted nothing more than to return to America, she knew she was enjoying a rare opportunity in Europe. In her own words, she "hung on as long as she could."[6]

While Douglas made the most of her remaining time in Paris, her personal life continued to be unsettled, at best. During her travels she had met and become fond of a fellow Red Cross volunteer, a man she would later identify only as "Frederick." According to Douglas, while she cared for Frederick's feelings, she was still in love with Andy. Frederick, however, fell in love with her and asked her to marry him. At first, she told him no, but then, when she saw how he, in her words, "began to mourn around," she agreed to marry him, "if only to make him happy."[7]

Unfortunately, neither Douglas's autobiography nor the collection of her papers on file at the University of Miami in Florida sheds any more light on her feelings at this time. As a consequence, we're forced to surmise and draw conclusions from the only hint she did leave, her declaration that she agreed to his proposal "only to make him happy."

Why would Douglas say she said she would become the wife of a man she had no intention of marrying? Her comment seems, at first glance, almost too shallow to believe. However, if we take that statement at face value, it seems obvious that Douglas was still bedeviled by feelings of insecurity and worthlessness stemming from her abandonment by her father. It seems these feelings made her afraid of rejection, so afraid that she would even promise marriage to a man she did not love rather than run the risk of losing his friendship.

In any event, when Douglas returned to America in late 1919, she was engaged to Frederick. Luckily for both Frederick and Douglas, she found the courage to break off the relationship not long after her return.

Meanwhile, after an absence of about sixteen months, Douglas was anxious to get back to Miami.

However, she decided to visit her grandmother, grandfather, and aunt before returning to the city she now considered her home. It must have been difficult for her to return to the home that had been so filled with pain when she was a girl, to see again her mother's room and to remember the loneliness of her childhood. All told, the visit could not have been very pleasant. Douglas's grandmother and aunt were disappointed that she was returning to Miami and, no doubt, made their continuing dislike of her father plain.

Still, Douglas must have been glad she'd stopped to visit. Her grandfather, who'd taken her and her mother in when Douglas was a little girl, lived only a short time after her visit before dying at the age of ninety-four.

It was January of 1920 by the time Douglas arrived back in South Florida. At that time her father and stepmother were living in a small apartment awaiting the completion of a new home not far from what is now downtown Miami. Since their apartment had no room for Douglas, she moved in with friends she'd made before leaving for France. She immediately started her new duties as assistant editor at the *Herald*. One of her jobs was writing a regular editorial column called The Galley. This column gave her a chance to write with her own voice, commenting about local politics, about Florida's landscape, the environment, and the plight of women in South Florida, all subjects that would occupy an increasingly important place in her life over the years.

Andy immediately moved back into her life during this period. Sadly, like many veterans of war, the young man Douglas loved had been—in a real sense—wounded by his experiences in combat. He was, in Douglas's words, "battered . . . exhausted from fighting in the war, and progressively unhappy."[8] It did not help matters at all that while Douglas was earning a man's salary of about $30 a week as the *Herald's* assistant editor, Andy had a difficult time finding work that made him happy.

Once again, Douglas's desire for a steady relationship with a man, for both love and companionship, was doomed. Depressed, unwilling to marry a woman who was employed and making more money than he was, Andy decided to move to a northern city to take a job he'd been offered by a friend. Though Douglas agreed that moving was the right thing for Andy to do, his departure left her, she said, "with the familiar sense of misery" she knew so well.[9]

As sad as the end of her romance was for Douglas, it proved to be a blessing. It forced her to take stock of herself again, as she had a few years earlier when her marriage to Kenneth Douglas came to an end. This time, though, Douglas realized that she really did not want to marry again. She did not really want to marry Andy, even though she loved him. Nor did she wish to marry anybody else. She came, she later said, to the realization that she did not wish to give up her own life for anyone else.

"I didn't want a normal family life," she said. "I wanted my own life in my own way. I was too interested in writing editorials and in writing my column. . . . To me, this was more important than getting tied up with a man."[10]

Back in
Florida,
Douglas's eyes
are opened to
the beauty
and history
of her adopted
city of
Miami.

While Douglas seems to have been confident about this decision to live alone, her writing gives at least one hint that she might later have come to regret this decision. In a brief journal entry she penned in 1930, a quote from the famous philosopher Bertrand Russell, she wrote: "Of all forms of caution, caution in love is perhaps the most fatal to true happiness."[11] We can only wonder at just what sadness and unhappiness Douglas—by that time firmly committed to living alone—was feeling when she wrote that entry.

In any event, the realization that she could be complete, if not necessarily happy, without a man in her life, freed Marjory Stoneman Douglas for the important work as an author, environmentalist, and activist that lay ahead for her.

Chapter Six

A Newspaper Woman

The Miami that Douglas returned to in 1920 was very different from the city she'd left just two years earlier. "The wonderful light, the incomparable bay and sea were the same," she said in a note written years after the fact. "The city was completely changed. There were more people, more buildings, more business."[1]

The small town she'd known on the Miami River had doubled in size. "Everyone was making money, buying and selling land, much of which they never saw."[2]

In fact, Miami was in the earliest stages of what would become one of the wildest real estate booms in history. The city's population—which had risen from about 5,500 in 1910 to almost 30,000 in 1920—would continue soaring in the next decade, nearly quadrupling to more than 110,000.

There were many reasons for the boom that swept Miami—and, to a lesser degree, the rest of Florida—in the early 1920s. Automobiles, a novelty before World War I, were becoming common and so were well-paved roads. That meant people had mobility as never before. At the same time, most Americans were feeling good about themselves and their future in the wake of the war to end all wars. Times were good and many Americans were flush with cash thanks to a stock market that seemed destined to keep rising and rising.

Whatever the reasons, people came to Miami in droves. And once there, they bought real estate—land and homes and office buildings and apartments—as if money was no object. As prices rose, news of the Miami boom spread, and more and more people headed south to what seemed to be the pot of gold at the end of the rainbow.

About twenty years later, Douglas described those times in her book, *The Everglades, River of Grass:*

> The stock market was rising, but Miami real estate rose faster and more people talked about it and hurried to profit by it. Trains, boats, automobiles arrived jammed with people. Hotels and rooming houses were packed. Tourists slept on porches, in tents, on park benches.

The air was electric with talk of money. "Hundreds" became "thousands." "Millions" became a common word. Business lots, house lots, buildings, houses, tracts at the edge of the city, and tracts beyond tracts began to sell and resell as fast as the papers could be made out.[3]

While the boom would not reach its full frenzy until 1925, Miami and its beach were changing by 1920 when Douglas returned from Europe. Where once there had been just two casinos and a few houses on Miami Beach, the island about two miles off the coast of Miami, there were, in that year, dozens of buildings, hotels, and homes. Lincoln Road, a major thoroughfare that is now a shopping, restaurant, and entertainment center, had just been cleared and opened for traffic.

Miami itself was humming with activity. The city's first skyscraper, the ten-story McAllister Hotel, had just been constructed. The steel skeletons of other tall buildings were rising along what would become Biscayne Boulevard, the main thoroughfare along the city's bay front. As the city stretched its reach to the north, south, and west, subdivisions were being built as fast as land could be cleared.

It was an exciting time. Douglas—as assistant editor of what was rapidly becoming a major daily newspaper—was at the center of much of the action. She wrote an editorial column every day, and wrote articles about the city's social scene in addition to editing other writers' copy.

Thanks to her job she was able to meet and become

friendly with important people including David Fairchild, a famous botanist and the founder of a tropical garden that bears his name; Fairchild's wife, Marian, the daughter of Alexander Graham Bell; and Ruth Bryan Owens, William Jennings Bryan's daughter, who ultimately became the first woman to represent Florida in the U.S. Congress.

In the early 1920s, Douglas led a full social life. Though she apparently did not date regularly, she loved music and dancing and often went to dances at hotels and at outdoor dance floors on Miami Beach. Later in her life, she said she wished she had a dollar for every mile she danced in those days.

If Douglas missed having a man in her life, she gave no real hint of it in her autobiography. Still, there must have been times when she thought of Andy or of Frederick. She must have wondered what her life would be like if she was married. There must have been times, too, when she simply felt lonely. It would have been perfectly natural for her to have those thoughts and feelings as she sat alone listening to music while loving couples danced together nearby or while she sat on a secluded beach, looking at the full moon's reflection on the waters of a dark ocean.

If Douglas felt lonely it was because she missed companionship, not because of unfulfilled passion. As far as she was concerned at that point in her life, sex was of no importance. By her own account, she was celibate both before and after her marriage to Kenneth Douglas . . . and she never missed the sex she'd enjoyed so much during her brief marriage. "People don't seem to realize that the energy that goes into sex, all the emotion that surrounds it, can be well employed in other ways,"[4] she said late in her life.

In fact, Douglas poured all her energy into her work in the years immediately following her return from Europe. In addition to her writing, she became involved for the first time in an effort to save the vast watery, grassy area of South Florida known as the Everglades. Using her newspaper column as what President Theodore Roosevelt called a "bully pulpit," she wrote about the importance of setting aside at least a portion of the Everglades as a national park. She also joined David Fairchild and other influential Miamians on a committee that worked actively to save the region most Floridians know as the 'Glades.

Douglas admitted that when she began writing about the Everglades and working to save it she knew little about the region. Of course, most of the Everglades was completely inaccessible except by canoe. A two-lane road known as the Tamiami Trail, crossing the Everglades to link Tampa on the west coast of Florida with Miami on the east, was under construction, but far from completed.

To learn about the Everglades, Douglas and a group of her friends would rise before daybreak and drive west to the end of that road. There they'd build a fire, cook breakfast, and watch as the sun rose. While Douglas was charmed by the Everglades in the early 1920s, she was not yet enthralled, she was not yet ready to make the Everglades a full-time cause.

Meanwhile, Douglas was also interested in social issues and used her column to bring about change. In 1923, Douglas learned that a young man named Martin Tabert, a vagrant from North Dakota, had been arrested and jailed in one of Florida's brutal prison labor camps. While in prison, he was beaten to death.

Shocked by Tabert's story, Douglas wrote a poem she called "Martin Tabert of North Dakota Is Walking Florida Now." Published in the *Miami Herald* and then picked up by several other newspapers, the poem read:

> *Martin Tabert of North Dakota is walking Florida*
> *   now.*
> *O children, hark to his footsteps coming, for he's*
> *   walking soft and slow.*
> *Through the piney woods and the cypress hollows,*
> *A wind creeps up and it's him it follows.*
> *Martin Tabert of North Dakota is walking Florida*
> *   now.*
> *O children, the tall pines stood and heard him*
> *   when he was moaning low.*
> *The other convicts, they stood around him,*
> *When the length of the black strap cracked and*
> *   found him.*
> *Martin Tabert of North Dakota. And he's walking*
> *   Florida now.*
> *The whip is still in the convict camps, for Florida's*
> *   stirring now.*
> *Children, from Key West to Pensacola you can hear*
> *   the great wind go.*

The wind that he roused when he lay dying,
The angry voice of Florida crying,
"Martin Tabert of North Dakota,
Martin Tabert of North Dakota,
Martin Tabert of North Dakota,
You can rest from your walking now."[5]

After its publication, this poem attracted a great deal of attention, so much that beatings were abolished in labor camps. Douglas was proud of the poem and the fact that she played a part in ending prison camp beatings, even though conditions in the camps remained inhumane. "I think that's the single most important thing I was ever able to accomplish as a result of something I've written," she said.[6]

As shocked as Douglas was by Tabert's story, she was no less shocked by the treatment of African Americans in what was then called "Colored Town" in Miami. Residents lived in poverty, without running water and toilets. She knew that keeping Miami's blacks in poverty and filth was harmful not just to the black residents of the city but also to the whites. "You can only keep a person in the gutter by getting into the gutter yourself," she said, adding that "that was exactly what happened" in Miami.[7]

Wanting to improve living conditions for the black residents of the city, she started a fund to supply milk to needy families. On that project she had her father's blessing. She was able to use her newspaper column to ask for donations.

Soon, though, she realized that Miami's poor blacks

needed more than milk. They needed family counseling, legal aid, training so they could find good jobs, and low-interest loans. When she tried to enlist her father's help—and through him, that of the *Herald*—he put his foot down. As far as he, and in fact, most men and women were concerned in the early 1920s, ideas like Douglas's were radical and dangerous. This difference of opinion led to friction between Douglas and Frank Stoneman.

In early 1924, Douglas had what she described as a "nervous breakdown." She was exhausted. Sometimes her mind would go blank as she sat rigid, unable to move. Finally, one night, confused and unable to sleep, she became, in own her words, "unhinged a little."[8] In the middle of the night she left her father's house, where she was living at the time, and began aimlessly wandering the dark and deserted streets of Miami.

Justifiably alarmed when he found out his daughter had been wandering the streets all night, Frank Stoneman called a doctor who told Douglas she was worn out by work and advised her to leave her job at the *Miami Herald*.

Douglas took the doctor's advice. While her departure from the newspaper upset her father—who had hoped she would someday take over as the paper's editor—it was not entirely unwelcome as far as Douglas was concerned. By that time, she was growing tired of the newspaper business with its daily grind and routine.

Even before she left the *Herald*, Douglas had started earning some extra money writing short stories for magazines. A few of those stories had been published in *Ainslee's*, a popular magazine in the 1920s.

In the wake of her breakdown, she decided to try her hand at writing stories full time. Douglas's life was about to move in a direction that would prepare her for her most important work.

Included with Douglas's collected papers at the University of Miami are a series of diaries she kept from early 1924 until 1930. These diaries are tiny notebooks—small enough to carry in a shirt pocket or purse—filled with page after page of Douglas's jotted notes, most often written with a fountain pen, but occasionally in pencil.

For the most part, these notes are the typical jottings of a writer, kind of "word-doodles." There are quotes from other writers, long lists of words, lists of names she might use in stories, half thought-out plots, and brief scenes that were obviously ideas she had for stories.

Occasionally, though, Douglas's notes give us at least a glimpse into her state of mind at this period. On August 10, 1924, for example, she wrote: "Marriage as a goal is passive, unless coincidentally with the idea of marriage a woman has constructively developed her personality in such fashion as to be a powerful directing force in the life of the man she marries."[9]

Though this passage was not original, and was copied from a book she did not identify, it still offers a tantalizing peek into Douglas's state of mind as she left the *Herald* to strike out on her own. At the very least, it tells us that the subject of marriage was in her thoughts. Was she wistful? Did she at some level wish she had "constructively developed" her personality to a point

April 12.

~~Smith and Son~~
Brown and Son.
Father and son
and other women
shipwrecked —
? Something of
which the woman
clings more than
that.
Play for Katharine
Cornell —
Woman — it is
nothing
Woman clings

to her independence
more than that —
Father — protection for
son.
Son — ~~love of~~ Youth
Thoughtless and insisting
on natural and
temporary.

Add a dark hand   ?

or rather — Woman as
symbol of sex — not
as important as anyone
thinks.

*A page from Douglas's 1926 diary in which
she is puzzling over a story idea*

where she could have married? Or was she content that she did not have to worry at all about entering what would have been a "passive" relationship?

Of course we'll never know. What we do know is that Douglas was about to enter a period of her life that was to be simultaneously painful and exciting, creatively challenging, and rewarding. She was entering a time that would prepare her fully to write what would be one of the most celebrated environmental books of all time.

Chapter Seven

Stories

Douglas had saved some money during her time at the *Herald* when she was living in her father and stepmother's new home. So she had few money worries when she first left the newspaper to become a freelance writer. Unlike many men and women who try to earn money writing, she had the freedom to concentrate on her creative work.

"I could work in my room and write all day and nobody bothered me," she said, adding that she was able to recover from the nervous breakdown she suffered before leaving newspaper work "by being quiet, sleeping late, and by beginning to write short stories."[1]

For most of the next two decades, Douglas devoted the lion's share of her creative energy to writing magazine stories. In those days short fiction published in magazines and in major newspapers enjoyed the kind of popularity television does in the twenty-first century. Still, many would-be writers struggled for years without ever making a sale to a major publication. Freelance writing was—and still is—a field where failure is much more common than success. Douglas, however, had proven her abilities as a fiction writer—at least in a small way—by publishing a few stories while she was still working for her father at the *Herald*. She soon proved that she could find success in a broader market, with a much larger audience.

In 1924, the first year of her career as a freelance writer, five of her stories and one long novella were published. In the years between 1925 and 1943 about fifty additional stories made it into print. Many of the short stories Douglas wrote in those years were published by *The Saturday Evening Post*, one of the most popular magazines in America, and one of the best paying.

In the years from 1924 to the early 1940s, Douglas did not limit herself to writing fiction. She also wrote several nonfiction articles, including a series about the history of piracy, and one about the Everglades. In her heart, though, Douglas loved writing short stories, not only because of the creative challenge such writing gave her, but also because she did not have to spend long hours in research the way she did when writing nonfiction. "It was easier to write fiction," she said. "For me it was a perfect job."[2]

Almost every story Douglas wrote was about Florida. Some dealt with the Miami land boom that continued until 1926 when the city was ravaged by a killer hurricane. Others had to do with the rough-and-tumble nature of Florida life in the early years of the twentieth century, when gunrunning and smuggling were still commonplace. Almost all of her stories used nature and the environment as characters that were every bit as important to the story as the hero or antagonist.

Interestingly, several of Douglas's heroines were unmarried women from New England, strong women who were forced to deal with hard times and difficult circumstances in South Florida. Douglas may well have seen some of herself in these characters, characters who struggled alone to overcome life's problems. And, in her success as well as theirs, she found something to cheer. "It was her grim New England feeling that nothing was any good until it had demonstrated its ability to live through hardship," she wrote about one of those characters.[3]

Over time, as Douglas's reputation as a writer grew, she was paid as much as $1,200 for a single story, very good money in the 1920s and 1930s—a time when the average American wage earner made only about $750 per year.

Her stories were also praised by critics. Two—"He Man," a story published in the *Saturday Evening Post* in mid-1927, and "The Peculiar Treasure of Kings," published in the *Post* later that same year—were awarded prizes in the O. Henry Memorial Award contest, held each year to honor the best short fiction published in the United States.

Even as she found success as a short-story writer, Douglas was tortured by doubts about her creative abilities, particularly in early 1926, when she went through a period, as almost all writers do, when her work was not going well and sales dried up.

Her doubts and fears made their way onto the pages of the tiny diaries she kept during those early years of her freelance career.

"Everything is just a little better than bad," she wrote on May 1, 1926, after several of her stories were turned down by editors. "But what to do[?] Where to find the right thing [to write?] Am filled with a vast lack of self-confidence. . . . I only know that I can't write pot-boilers [inferior stories, written only to make money] in this frame of mind and I don't want to write anything but the best I can right now. But how can one tell in the heart of one's desire, just what will be slowly and gravely beautiful[?]"

The pain she felt was almost visible on the pages of her diary. Writing, she said, was "like tearing one's way through concrete."[4]

During this same period, when her work did not sell or sold slowly, Douglas also fretted about money. Her worries were compounded by the fact that, starting not long after she left the *Herald*, she had to meet the costs of building a cottage, a home for herself, on a small lot she'd purchased in Coconut Grove, south of downtown Miami.

Though Douglas was comfortable living with her father and stepmother, she knew—at the age of thirty-four—that it was time for her to be on her own. She loved Coconut Grove, a place she described as "a kind of half garden, half community."[5] Some time in 1925, she hired a contractor to build a house on her tiny plot of land.

Douglas borrowed money to pay for her little slice of land and to build a house. The first contractor she hired—probably one of a number of less-than-reputable builders operating in South Florida during the real-estate boom—somehow managed to run away with the money she'd borrowed to pay for the construction of her home. That meant she had to pay for the house, over time, using money she scraped together from the sale of her stories.

Slowly, the cottage took shape. It was (and still is) an unpretentious little home, looking like a quaint English country cottage somehow misplaced under the palm trees and gumbo-limbo trees of South Florida. The cottage—with plenty of windows to capture cool breezes and a mushroom-shaped roof—was basically one large open room where Douglas wrote and read and entertained guests and spent most of her time. Off to one side of this large room was a tiny sleeping area, large enough for a twin bed and little else, and an equally tiny storage area that was also used for cooking.

Soon after Douglas's cottage was finished, Miami was devastated by one of the worst hurricanes ever to strike South Florida. She was out of town on the night of September 17 when the killer storm struck. It is estimated that wind speeds exceeded 120 miles per hour.

*Douglas, on the left, entertains her
friends in her Coconut Grove yard.*

The storm surge—a wall of water pushed ashore by the storm—was powerful enough to flatten trees and homes and other buildings on Miami Beach. It drove a five-masted schooner ashore, high and dry in the middle of Biscayne Road, about a half mile from open water. All told, the storm killed about four hundred people. Douglas's new house, built on a ridge about six and a half feet above sea level, survived the storm, though all its windows were blown out and seaweed and debris were washed inside by the exceptionally high tide.

At times during this period, as Douglas kept writing stories and struggled to make ends meet, the financial pressure bothered her. In February 1927, not long after she moved into the cottage, she wrote that she was "still in financial difficulties." However, she added, she was "more able to take them [her difficulties] more lightly; although tomorrow or next day the shell of protection may crash in. . . ."[6]

Eventually, Douglas came to look on the building of her cottage as one of the most important things she accomplished in the early years of her career as a writer. The tiny home on a ridge outside what was then metropolitan Miami became not only her headquarters but also a place of refuge. She filled it with books she loved and bits of unmatched furniture she got from friends or saved from the junk heap. She lived a very simple life, sleeping late in the morning and working until late at night, writing story after story.

In this period of her life, as Douglas reached the age of forty, it must have appeared to all who knew her that she had put the pain of her early life behind her. However, there are some signs that she continued to be troubled by the loneliness and self-doubt that had marked her as a girl and young woman.

In late 1929 she must have been thinking of that loneliness or perhaps of love . . . or the lack of love . . . in her life when she wrote a letter to Dr. Smith Ely Jelliffe, a New York physician, probably a psychologist or psychiatrist. While that letter is lost, Dr. Jelliffe's answer, dated January 14, 1930, makes it clear that she asked him for advice about how to rid herself of what she saw in herself as a "father fixation."

After writing about the nature of such a fixation, Dr. Jelliffe gave Douglas a way that she might deal with what she obviously saw as a problem. "One is less interested in getting rid of a fixation," the doctor had written, "than in shifting its load and changing the direction of the energy from . . . destructive to creative ends."[7]

Of course, there is no way to determine Douglas's state of mind in 1929 or in 1930 with any certainty. However, from other evidence, it seems at least plausible that Douglas took the doctor's advice and started focusing more energy on her creative work and less on worrying about the past and how her relationship—or lack of a relationship—with her father had shaped her life.

At the very least, this might explain why Douglas seems to have stopped keeping detailed, somewhat self-absorbed diaries in 1930, not long after she received the doctor's letter. In fact, there is a gap in the diaries included in her papers from mid-1930 until 1947. And, when she began keeping diaries again, they contained no references to the kind of pain she experienced or the kind of questions she asked of herself in the 1920s.

At the same time, if Douglas did, as Dr. Jelliffe suggested, cease worrying about the past while focusing more energy on her writing, it helps explain why the 1930s were the most creative period of Douglas's life, a time when she wrote—and published—one article and short story after another.

Meanwhile, during these productive years, Douglas continued working, in small ways, to improve the lives of African Americans in South Florida. When she and a group of her friends discovered that blacks living in Coconut Grove had no sewers or freshwater, they pushed legislation to require the installation of indoor plumbing in all houses in Dade County (the home county of Miami and Coconut Grove). Douglas then suggested the establishment of a loan fund to enable black men and women to borrow money to build bathrooms in their homes.

Of course, Douglas also had a social life. She kept her old friends and made new ones. She went back to Taunton frequently to visit her still-living relatives until 1938 when her Aunt Fanny, the aunt who had helped finance her Wellesley education, died. At that time, the big old house in which Douglas had grown up was empty. She sold the house and never returned to Taunton.

Douglas also remained close to her father and stepmother, visiting three or four times each week. Usually, she and her father would play checkers and talk about books and argue good-naturedly about literature.

In February 1941, Frank Stoneman died at the age of eighty-four. While doctors said he died of complications of kidney stones, Douglas felt sure he simply lost his desire to live. The thought of another world war was difficult for him and, according to Douglas, he said that he "couldn't take it."[8]

Frank Stoneman's death devastated Douglas. For the second time, she suffered what she described as a "psychosis," and was found by her neighbors wandering the streets near her home at night, dressed in a nightgown, screaming.[9]

Luckily Douglas found treatment that enabled her to quickly recover and a compassionate doctor who guided her back to health. As terrible as this time was for Douglas, this episode in her life marked a real turning point in her life. Perhaps because her father, to whom she had felt so tied for most of her life, was dead, she felt somehow renewed, despite her grief. "It was the end of my immature life, if one can say that at the age of fifty-one, and the beginning of a new maturity," she said later.[10]

According to the *Miami Herald*, Frank Stoneman's estate amounted to $11,330 in cash, an automobile worth $150, and about $50 worth of books.[11] Thanks to her portion of this small inheritance, Douglas was able to begin work on a novel and turn her back on short-story writing. Though she loved writing stories, the market was changing in the early 1940s. Magazines were publishing fewer and fewer stories. Equally important, readers were enamored of the new sparse writing style of Ernest Hemingway and other members of a new generation of authors. Douglas's writing—somewhat wordy and florid—was no longer in style, or in demand.

While Douglas—like many short-story writers—had long dreamed of writing a longer work of fiction, she found it difficult work when, in the months following her father's death, she first turned her hand to writing a novel. After some twenty years of writing short stories, she had a tendency to turn each chapter into a story of its own, with a climax.

Luckily for her, she spent only about six months struggling on a novel when an old friend, Hervey Allen, came to visit her in her Coconut Grove house. Allen was a famous writer, the author of *Anthony Adverse*, a best-selling book that had been published in 1933. In 1941 or 1942 (much later in her life Douglas wasn't sure of the date), when he came to visit her, he had been named editor in charge of a series of books, the *Rivers of America* series, being published by a major New York publishing house. As editor, Allen hired well-known writers to create books about the Hudson, the Illinois, the Mississippi, and so on. He asked Douglas a fateful question. He asked if she would write a book about the Miami River.

Douglas almost laughed out loud. "Hervey," she said, "you can't write a book about the Miami River. It's only about an inch long." But then, as Douglas later said, she realized what she was doing.

"(W)hen a publisher visits your house and asks you

to write something, you don't let him go casually," she said.[12] Thinking quickly, she suggested that since the Miami River was connected to the Everglades, perhaps the river might be part of that vast watershed. She asked Allen if she could somehow show that the Everglades fed the river perhaps she could do a book about the whole ecosystem.

Allen didn't even hesitate. He approved her idea on the spot.

"There," Douglas later said, "on a writer's whim and an editor's decision, I was hooked with the idea that would consume me the rest of my life."[13]

It was an idea . . . and a writing project . . . that would lead to worldwide fame for Douglas.

Chapter Eight

The River of Grass

In 1942, when Marjory Stoneman Douglas set out to write a book about the Miami River and the Everglades, she knew very little about the vast watershed that covers much of southern Florida. Twenty years earlier she and her friends had gone fishing in a canal that bordered the road that eventually became the Tamiami Trail, a highway running through the Everglades from the east coast of Florida to the west. She'd stepped around water moccasins that sunned themselves in the road, stood transfixed watching seemingly endless flights of white ibises soaring overhead, and been struck by the beauty of what she described as "the untouched Everglades lying all beyond under the sun."[1]

As a journalist, Douglas had been interested enough in the Everglades to editorialize about its importance. In 1927 she joined the committee that was established to try to save at least a part of the 'Glades from development. She'd even written a couple of articles about the Everglades as a freelance writer. But she'd never really studied it, certainly not in enough depth to write an entire book about it.

In fact, Douglas spent little time in the Everglades before she wrote her book. "What I knew about the Everglades . . . [was] that it was there. . . . I'd been out in the Everglades no more than 20 times," she said later.[2] She and the Everglades, she explained, had the kind of friendship that did not require "constant physical contact."[3]

Douglas was a good reporter, though. She knew how to do research, how to dig for the facts and history she needed. She started her research by meeting with Garald Parker, Florida's state hydrologist, the man in charge of water conservation and usage, at his office in Miami. From Parker, she later said, she learned that the Everglades was not a swampy wasteland. Instead, he told her, it was actually a body of fresh, shallow water that moved, almost imperceptibly, beneath a carpet of saw grass, inexorably south and west from Lake Okeechobee in mid-southern Florida. It emptied into the Gulf of Mexico and Florida Bay, in a region known as the Ten Thousand Islands.

"Do you think I could get away with calling it the river of grass?" she asked the hydrologist.[4] He answered that she could. At that moment Douglas had discovered not just the title of her book, but also the book's central creative idea.

More than forty years later, Douglas remembered Parker with fondness and gratitude. She was happy to give him credit for his contribution to her book and her success. "I will never forget how kind Gerry was to a wild woman who had to write a book on a subject about which she knew nothing," she said in a letter written in 1985.[5]

Indeed, Garald Parker's contribution to Douglas's work was huge. Without his guidance, she might never have identified the Everglades as the river of grass. Years after the publication of her book, Art Marshall, a friend and fellow conservationist, told Douglas that those three simple words—"river of grass"—changed the popular perception of the Everglades.

Douglas spent roughly four years doing research for the book that eventually established her reputation as a writer and changed the way people thought of what most had considered nothing more than a useless swamp. During her research, Douglas was helped not just by Parker but also by several other individuals, including John Goggin, a writer-historian who provided invaluable research material about the earliest residents of South Florida, the Tekesta and Calusa Indians.

In the course of her research, she came to know, she said, not just the Everglades, but the entire body of flowing freshwater known as the Kissimmee-

Okeechobee-Everglades basin. She learned that rainfall fed and nourished this basin, including the Kissimmee River, Lake Okeechobee, and the Everglades itself. She learned that most of this rainfall, which keeps South Florida green and alive, comes from the Everglades itself. "In the rainy season, water evaporating from [the Everglades] wetlands soars up as vapor to build cumulus clouds and as winds blow northward [this water] is released again as rain over South Florida."[6]

As she studied the Everglades, Douglas saw clearly that the environmental health of all South Florida depended on the health of the 'Glades. She became convinced that the survival of South Florida depended on the freshwater flow of the river of grass. "Drain the Everglades," she said, "and South Florida would become a semitropical desert."[7]

During her research, Douglas read government reports that convinced her that politicians were doing a terrible job of managing what she came to realize was one of the most valuable natural resources in the world. She read the history of the 'Glades and learned how the region had been imperiled for more than a century. She visited the Everglades more frequently and became passionate about her subject.

At some point during her research, Douglas began writing her now-famous book. She sat at the worktable in her tiny, high-ceilinged cottage. Though, as a reporter, she knew how to type using two fingers, she chose to write the first draft of her book using a fountain pen on lined yellow paper.

In the rush to develop Florida there was no consideration for protecting natural resources. People thought of the Everglades as a swamp to be filled in.

"I wanted to get away from that newspaper thing," she said, "and writing it in longhand made me look at things in a different way."[8]

Only a few pages of her original, handwritten manuscript—now crisp and fragile with age—are on file with the rest of her papers at the Richter Library at the University of Miami in Miami, Florida. These pages show that Douglas wrote with little hestitation. Her handwriting is strong, sure, with thick vertical strokes that appear almost angry, as if she'd pressed her pen hard against the paper. There are almost no cross outs, only a few corrections scattered through the pages she wrote.

In her strong hand, Douglas wrote: "There are no other Everglades in the world." Those words, the opening words of *Everglades: River of Grass* are famous. Many Floridians, and even environmentalists who have never seen the Everglades, know them by heart and use them as a kind of anthem. The words that follow are slightly less well known, but they give testimony to Douglas's love for the Everglades, and her realization of just how important the region is.

The Everglades, she wrote: ". . . are, they have always been, one of the unique regions of the earth, remote, never wholly known. Nothing anywhere else is like them. . . . The miracle of the light pours over the green and brown expanse of saw grass and of water, shining and slow-moving below, the grass and water that is the meaning and the central fact of the Everglades of Florida. It is a river of grass."[9]

All told, it took Douglas five years to complete her book. During that period she bent her life to meet the needs of her writing to a remarkable degree, particularly for a woman in the 1940s. Typically she worked late at night, often after going out to dinner with friends. Then, as quiet settled on the streets around her cottage, she would sit at her desk, writing in longhand, and then, later, rewriting, pecking away at her typewriter with two fingers until early morning. Falling into bed when many people rise to begin work, she would then sleep until the sun was high over the Everglades that lay to the west of Miami. If she needed to, she would nap in the afternoon.

At this point in her life, Douglas was what she called "a writing woman." She was writing about a topic she cared about deeply, creating a book she knew was important. Though there must have been periods when the words, the writing, did not come easily for her, she must have known she was writing well, crafting a book she later called her "most ambitious and important project."[10]

In her book Douglas told the story of the Everglades through its people and its wildlife. She wrote of the Calusa and the Mayaimi and the Tekesta Indians who lived on the fringes of the Everglades and fished and hunted in its grassy interior long before the first Europeans came to Florida. She told how those Native Americans had given the region a "perfect and poetic" name when they called it Pa-hay-okee, an Indian word that means "Grassy Water."[11] She wrote of the first Europeans who visited the interior of Florida, and of efforts to subdue the Seminole Indians who took refuge in the inhospitable depths of the 'Glades, hoping to avoid the whites who wanted to move them from their lands and who were willing to wage war to get land.

Douglas detailed the history of man's efforts to build dikes and drain the river of grass, to make the land arable. She told of the damage done to the vast watershed by land-hungry men. They built canals to take the water away and surrounded Lake Okeechobee with a dike that stopped the flow of water from the lake through the saw-grass river. Even as she was writing her book, the U.S. Army Corps of Engineers—in response to cries from developers worried about flooding—carved up much of the Everglades with 1,000 miles of levees, or dikes, 1,000 miles of canals, and 150 pumping stations and other buildings.

River of Grass was poetic and powerful in ways that none of her other writing ever was. She wrote of clouds that "stand like Alps of pure rose and violet and ice-gray against the ultimate blue" of the sky;[12] of rain that falls in "long straight . . . lines [that] blow and curve from the sagging underbelly of the sky in steely wires or long-trailing veils of wet. . . ."[13]

She wrote of the creatures of the 'Glades: alligators and bears and deer and otters and raccoons and, of course, the birds. Douglas seemed to have a special place in her heart for the birds, for the white pelicans that float "like a snowbank on a reef" in shallow water; and tiny sandpipers and sanderlings that "rise in clouds from the water meadows"; and herons and roseate spoonbills and white ibises that fly across the landscape in a "huge sweeping, turning, flashing circle."[14]

John Rothchild, who interviewed Douglas for two hundred hours when he helped her write her memoirs in 1989, said the Everglades turned her into a poet. Writing about a subject she loved, he said, "made her lyrical that one time."[15]

It was late 1946 or early 1947 when Douglas finally finished her book and sent it off to her editor. According to the terms of her contract, *River of Grass* was supposed to be about 120,000 words in length. The book she submitted was 20,000 words longer than that. Her editor asked her to cut the extra words. Douglas, like writers before and after her, found cutting words from her manuscript difficult. "It was one of the worst jobs I ever had," she said. "I took those words out almost one-by-one. . . ."[16] Though the work was difficult, she stuck with it. Pages of her original manuscript, on file with her other papers, show how she toiled. A word is crossed out here . . . a sentence or paragraph there. And on the first page of the rough draft of each chapter is a notation of how many words remained after her careful editing.

Eventually Douglas cut 19,000 words from her book. She then wired her editor. "Cut 19,000. Refuse to cut another word. If you don't agree, I withdraw book from publication." Her editor took the book as it was.[17]

Douglas's publisher—Holt, Rinehart & Winston— printed 7,500 copies of *River of Grass* in November 1947. By Christmas Day, that entire first printing had been sold—a remarkable sales record for a nonfiction book by a relatively little-known writer. Holt immediately printed 5,000 more copies. Meanwhile, *Reader's Digest* magazine bought the first chapter and printed it, then reprinted it in foreign languages for editions around the world.

Everglades: River of Grass was, for a nonfiction book, a major success. In a review, fellow Floridian Marjorie Kinnan Rawlings, author of *The Yearling*, called it a "beautiful and bitter, sweet and savage book."[18] She praised it further in a personal letter, calling it a "magnificent piece of creative work."[19] Environmentalist Nat Reed, who lives in South Florida on the fringe of the Everglades, said it was "absolutely damn near poetry."[20]

Other critics, including John Hersey, the famous novelist, agreed. Writing in a review in the *New York Herald Tribune*, Hersey said Douglas's imagery was "dazzling," and went on to say she brought to her writing "an organization and discipline that approach poetic form."[21]

Douglas herself was more down to earth in describing her work. Later in her life, when asked by a journalist how she was able to combine such sweeping poetry with journalism, she answered simply. "I went out there. I looked. I came back and wrote about what I saw."[22]

On December 6, 1947, soon after the publication of *River of Grass*, Douglas was invited to attend a special ceremony at Everglades City, on the edge of the river of grass. At that ceremony, President Harry Truman formally set aside about 1.5 million acres, or roughly one

President Harry Truman dedicates the
Everglades as a national park.

third of the Everglades, as a national park. Many people believe that the establishment of Everglades National Park was a direct result of Douglas's book. She herself, however, said the fact that the park was created at about the same time as the publication of her book was simply a matter of coincidence. At the same time, she gave credit to many people who were much more active in the move to save the Everglades than she was. Among those she credited were Ruth Bryan Owen, her old friend and the daughter of William Jennings Bryan, and Ernest Coe, the man who first dreamed of turning the Everglades into a national park.

As Douglas sat in the audience on that December day, she had reason to feel both proud and pleased. On the one hand, she had published a book that was, by that time, already selling well, a book that would establish her as a writer of note. On the other hand, at least part of the Everglades she loved was being protected, or so it seemed at that time.

But Douglas, then fifty-seven years of age, was not about to rest on her laurels. In fact, her career as a writer—and as an environmentalist—had barely begun. The woman who was born in the nineteenth century when Benjamin Harrison was president in the White House, was destined to keep working, and gaining fame for herself, for close to five more decades.

Chapter Nine

The Lady of the Everglades

The success of Everglades: River of Grass gave Marjory Stoneman Douglas a degree of financial security she had never known before in her professional life. She no longer had to worry—as she had during her short-story writing career—about paying bills.

With money in her purse, she was able to pamper herself. She traveled west to visit parts of the United States she'd never seen before. She called on distant relatives she'd never met before, stopped briefly in Mexico, stayed in a lodge overlooking the Grand Canyon, and then returned home by way of New Orleans, Louisiana.

Like many people who had to struggle financially at some time in their lives, who know what it is like to worry about making ends meet, Douglas was not comfortable living the life of a high spender. From New Orleans, she returned to Miami to recover from what she called her "spending spree."[1]

Once back in the familiar comfort of her little cottage in Coconut Grove, surrounded by her books and by her friends, Douglas picked up the novel she had abandoned to write *River of Grass* and started working on it again. Soon, she was back in her writing routine.

Douglas's social life, in the late 1940s and 1950s, was busy. Though it seems that Douglas stopped keeping diaries in 1930, she started again in 1947, right around the time she finished *River of Grass*. Her diaries for this period of her life, however, are more like social calendars, containing one terse reminder after another about social events she planned to attend. She jotted entries in her clear, strong handwriting about planned dinners with friends, cocktail parties, swimming excursions to the beach, birthday parties, speaking engagements, meetings, and appointments.

"Dinner . . . cocktails . . . Nell's B'day party . . . ," read her entries for February 21, 1947. Notes for several days a few weeks later include: "Dinner Edith . . . Dr. Howard at Library . . . Dinner Anna Cox . . . Bus. + Prof. [Business and Professional] Women's Club, 8 P.M., YWCA . . . Drinks, Dicky, Oyster House [a local restaurant]."[2]

Occasionally, Douglas entertained a few friends at her Coconut Grove cottage, though these gatherings had to be kept small, considering the tiny size of the home and the fact that she had no kitchen to speak of. With just a hot plate and a tiny countertop baking oven, she rarely cooked, preferring to eat out. On these occasions, since Douglas never learned to drive a car and never had a driver's license, some friend would pick her up at her house and drive her to her destination.

Missing from her diaries from this period were the quotes from other writers, musings about her work, the often painful questions about life and love and the philosophical reflections that had filled page after page of her little notebooks in the 1920s. Though we can't know for sure, it seems safe to assume that by this time, in the sixth decade of Douglas's life, she had clearly defined herself as a writer and as a woman. She was sure of herself, confident in her beliefs. Her tortured questioning had come to an end or, at the very least, no longer took up so much of her time and energy.

Her life was not without difficulty, however. In the early 1950s, as Douglas worked on her novel, she had to cope with the truth that she was, as she would have said, no great shakes as a novelist. "For me," she said later, "it was a terrible struggle to write a novel. I'd had too much short-story writing to be comfortable with the form."[3]

Though she found it difficult to write long fiction, she kept working, writing, and editing. Ultimately, she finished her novel in 1951. That book, *Road to the Sun*, told the story of a family that bought land on the edge

The now-famous Marjory Stoneman
Douglas relaxing outside her Coconut
Grove home

of the Everglades and then got caught up in the land boom of the 1920s. Published in 1952, it did not sell well.

Unhappy working as a novelist, Douglas soon turned her attention back to writing nonfiction. As a published author, with a best-selling book to her credit, she was sought out by publishers. Over the next two and a half decades, in her sixties, seventies, and eighties, Douglas wrote several successful books including *Hurricane* (1958), a study of great storms through history; *The Key to Paris* (1961), a travel memoir; *Florida, the Long Frontier* (1967), a popular history of Florida; *The Joys of Bird Watching in Florida* (1969); and *Adventures in a Green World—the Story of David Fairchild and Barbour Lathrop* (1973), about two of South Florida's early pioneering botanists. She also wrote two books for younger readers, *Freedom River* (1953) and *Alligator Crossing* (1959).

While she worked on her books for young readers, Douglas discovered that she could produce about five thousand words weekly (about the length of two chapters in this book) by writing on Monday, Tuesday, and Wednesday. That meant she could take the rest of the week off to visit with friends, go to the beach at night, and, in her words, "play around."[4]

Even with time out for playing around, Douglas was able, in this period, to write about a dozen nonfiction articles for newspapers and magazines including *The New York Times*, *Saturday Review*, *Audubon* (the magazine of the Audubon Society), and *Ladies Home Journal*. In addition, she contributed chapters or introductions to several books about Florida's environment and history.

In the midst of all this writing, in the early 1960s, Douglas was offered a job as editor of the University of Miami Press. Though she was already seventy years old—a time when many people retire or think about retiring—Douglas was ready and willing to go to work full time. She quickly accepted the job offer.

As it turned out, her stint as editor of the publishing house affiliated with the university did not work out. With a limited budget, Douglas was unable to actually do much publishing. Somehow, she scraped together enough money to print three books before the press itself was allowed to die a graceful death.

In 1967, not long after Douglas finished writing *Florida, the Long Frontier*, she found herself without a major project to work on. Though she was then seventy-six years old, about to celebrate her seventy-seventh birthday, she was used to working, to producing books and articles. She wanted to start another book. Eventually, she decided she would write a biography of W. H. Hudson, a naturalist and the Victorian-era author of *Green Mansions*. Though no editor expressed interest in the book, and at least one tried to talk her out of the project, Douglas was determined to press on with what she almost certainly knew would be the last major book she would ever write.

Undaunted by what was a great lack of interest in her project, she sought and eventually obtained a small grant—about two thousand dollars—from the Wellesley Alumnae Association.

Thanks in large part to Douglas's reputation, Friends of the Everglades grew like a thundercloud building in the sky over the Everglades. Within a year, the organization had more than five hundred members, in another year, more than one thousand, and within a few more years, three thousand members from thirty-eight states.

As the group grew, Douglas became its most vocal representative, attracting members simply by the strength of her reputation and character.

"Douglas had for decades been a moral force in South Florida on issues of women's rights and civil rights and community affairs," Joe Browder said. With her on the side of the Everglades, the "pro-Everglades people held the high moral ground."[6]

Douglas made use of that high moral ground, speaking whenever and wherever an audience of any size would gather to hear her speak. She spoke to individuals she met when she was shopping, she spoke at public hearings and to government officials. "If they haven't heard me, it isn't my fault," she once said about her willingness to speak in public about her beloved Everglades.[7]

With the passage of time, as Friends of the Everglades grew, Douglas and the organization she founded worked tirelessly to protect the Everglades as much as possible. In her eighties and then in her nineties, Douglas was, in a real sense, the "Voice of the Everglades." She became an idol to several generations of environmentalists. She also became someone to be feared by those who would savage the Everglades.

Even state officials who often felt Douglas's anger respected her. In 1985, on her ninety-fifth birthday, the state of Florida named its new Department of Natural Resources Building in Tallahassee in her honor.

As Douglas aged—her hair growing whiter and what she described as "old-lady thin,"[8] her body more frail, her hearing deteriorating, and her vision failing until she could no longer see even the Everglades themselves—she took advantage of both her reputation and her status as an elderly lady worthy of respect. She was known for refusing to give up the floor once she took it to begin talking. "[N]obody can be rude to me, this poor little old woman," she said. "I can be rude to them, poor darlings, but they can't be rude to me."[9]

The truth be told, Douglas could be rude, or at the very least plainspoken almost to a fault, when the spirit moved her. Once, when talking about the U.S. Army Corps of Engineers, one of her favorite targets, she sarcastically said the engineers caused more environmental problems than they cured for a simple reason. "Their mommies obviously never let them play with mud pies," she said, "and so now they take it out on us by playing with cement."[10]

Working to protect the 'Glades would have been a full-time occupation for most eighty year olds. Not for Douglas, though. Even as she stumped and spoke, she also continued writing the biography of W. H. Hudson, which she had started in 1969. Though her eye problems grew worse until she became legally blind at about the age of eighty-five, she took time from her environmental efforts to make several trips—with the aid of friends who served as her "eyes"—to England and to Argentina to do research for her book.

Indeed, Douglas's life was almost as full in her nineties as it had been when she was younger. The fact that she could no longer see to read or write hardly slowed her at all. Undaunted, she used secretaries who helped her with research, correspondence, and with her creative writing.

"In spite of my bad eyesight I have been able to keep working because I have three very fine secretaries . . . ," she wrote in July 1985, "one for Friends of the Everglades, one for my personal interests, and one who helps me so much with the Hudson biography."[11]

She was also able to continue her lifelong love affair with books thanks to the Talking Books program sponsored by the Library of Congress. This program makes tape-recorded books available to vision-impaired individuals. Most days Douglas relaxed in the late afternoon, after she finished her work, with a glass of scotch and one of the books sent to her by the library. "I don't think I could live without them," she said of the books.[12] The scotch was another matter. "Can't say I like the taste of liquor," she said, "but I don't know anything else that does what it does for me."[13]

Still and always at the center of her life during this period was the battle to protect South Florida's environment. She was instantly recognizable with her white hair, tiny stature, thick glasses, straw hat, and pearls. She became famous in Florida, and, to a slightly lesser degree, outside the state, as "the Lady of the Everglades," "the Mother of the Everglades," even, in some circles, "the Grande Dame of the Everglades."

Perhaps it was the constant fighting to protect the environment that kept Douglas relatively vibrant and healthy as she celebrated one birthday after another into her tenth and then her eleventh decade of life. In any case, she seemed to enjoy the warfare. "It's a lot more fun to fight for something important than to fight for something unimportant," she said when asked about her devotion to the Everglades. "It's a lot more fun to fight for something than not to fight for anything."[14]

It was during this period, at the age of ninety-five, that Douglas started dictating her life story to Miami writer John Rothchild. After taping some two hundred hours of conversations with Douglas, Rothchild edited her words and created *Marjory Stoneman Douglas: Voice of the River*. This book, published in 1987, tells Douglas's story in the voice, as Rothchild said, of the person best qualified to tell her story—herself.

As the 1980s came to an end, and Douglas neared her one hundredth birthday, there must have been periods when she felt frustrated. In the four decades since she'd written *River of Grass*, and the almost twenty years since she'd founded Friends of the Everglades, little real headway had been made in guaranteeing the long-term health of the 'Glades. To be sure, some minor victories had been scored. In 1983, for example, Bob Graham, then governor of Florida, announced the establishment of a "Save our Everglades" program. A half-dozen years later, when Douglas was ninety-nine years of age, President George H.W. Bush ordered the Army Corps of Engineers to restore the Kissimmee River—part of the South Florida watershed—to its original curving course, undoing some of the damage that had been done almost thirty years earlier. At the same time, the president added more than 100,000 acres of wetlands to the Everglades National Park. But the fight to save the fragile ecosystem was a long way from a successful end. Even at the age of one hundred, Douglas was unable to rest on her laurels.

Asked if she was encouraged about the future of the Everglades, her answer was typically to the point. "I'm neither encouraged nor discouraged," she said. "The Everglades must be taken care of. There's a job to do and it must be done."[15]

On her one hundredth birthday on April 7, 1990, Douglas was honored with a party at a fancy hotel in Coral Gables, not far from her home. By that time she was confined to a wheelchair, totally blind and almost totally deaf. At an age reached by only a few men and women, Marjory Stoneman Douglas was still lively. Wearing a light suit and a string of pearls, she basked in the attention of well-wishers, smiling and nodding to friends she could no longer see.

Around the same time, Douglas was honored in an unusual way that must have pleased her when she learned of it. In a 1990 episode of the cartoon series *The Simpsons*, Lisa Simpson, the brainy, talented daughter, cited Marjory Stoneman Douglas as one of the three most influential women of the century.

"I needed somebody so redoubtable [awe-inspiring or formidable] you couldn't make fun of them," said George Meyer, who wrote the episode. "I needed somebody with integrity."[16]

At one hundred years of age, Marjory Stoneman Douglas was indeed a redoubtable, remarkable woman. She was a woman of integrity who had become a part of Florida's history during her lifetime. Still, though, her story was not over.

Chapter Ten

The River at Ebb

As Marjory Stoneman Douglas passed the one-hundredth year of her life, she began reluctantly but understandably to curtail her activities. Weakened and slowed by age, legally blind and almost deaf, she took a much less active role in Friends of the Everglades. In 1990, not long after she turned one hundred, she resigned from her post as the group's president. Around that time she also stopped working on her biography of W. H. Hudson. Though she had written thousands and thousands of words—enough to fill two volumes of a biography—cutting and editing the pages was simply more than she could accomplish at her age and with her blindness.

As the 1990s progressed, Douglas also cut back on her public appearances. Increasingly debilitated, she spent almost all her time at home. Though she no longer spoke at public meetings, she was willing to talk with fellow environmentalists, with friends who often dropped in to visit, and with newspaper and magazine interviewers who loved to quote her about protecting the Everglades and other environmental issues. In 1992, at the age of one hundred and two, she spoke to reporters about a proposal to redefine wetlands that some environmentalists warned might lead to increased development in the Everglades and create further damage to the region's ecosystem. The proposal, she said, "was a very dangerous thing."[1]

It became something of a custom for interviewers from Florida newspapers to write about Douglas every year on April 7, as she celebrated yet another birthday. The headlines for the articles they wrote each year were like exclamations of surprise. "Everglades Hero Turns 105," read the headline of an article in 1995.[2] "Everglades 'Grandmother' Douglas Turns 106," read another the next year.[3] Then, "Champion of Everglades Turns 107," read a third.[4] In the accompanying articles, the story of her life would be briefly told, her accomplishments would be catalogued, and she would be quoted about the importance of efforts to save the Everglades. After she turned 103, though, reporters who quoted her were forced to rely on old quotes, for at that time Douglas stopped giving interviews.

During the 1990s, Douglas continued gaining honors for her work as an environmentalist. A half dozen or so public schools in Florida were named in her honor. A Florida state law passed in 1991, supposedly designed to protect the Everglades, was named the Marjory Stoneman Douglas Everglades Protection Act in her honor. While Douglas was understandably pleased when Lawton Chiles, then the governor, visited her Coral Gables cottage to tell her of the law's passage, she later asked that her name be taken off the law when she discovered that it fell far short, in her estimation, of sufficiently protecting the wetlands. Eventually, after the law was changed to make it stronger, she was convinced to let it carry her name.

In November 1993, Douglas received what must be considered the greatest honor of her long and honor-filled life. In a special ceremony in the East Room of the White House, she was awarded the Presidential Medal of Freedom by President Bill Clinton. This medal is the highest award that can be given to a civilian, the equivalent of the U.S. military's Medal of Honor. As the president approached her, Douglas rose from her wheelchair so he could fasten the gold medal with a white star on a blue ribbon around her neck.

A citation accompanying the award said Douglas's work to protect and restore the Everglades "enhanced our nation's respect for our precious environment by reminding all of us of nature's delicate balance."

Douglas receives the Presidential Medal of Freedom from President Bill Clinton

Referring to Douglas as "the Grandmother of the 'Glades," President Clinton said that "long before there was an Earth Day" she had "inspired generations of conservationists, environmentalists and preservationists." He went on to tell Douglas that anytime he heard anyone speak of the wonders and powers of Mother Nature, "I'll be thinking about you."[5]

While she was in Washington, D.C., for the presentation ceremony, Douglas, accompanied by several friends from Florida, spent one night in the visitors' quarters of the White House, was a guest at the signing ceremony for the gun-control law known as the "Brady Bill," and was treated to a tour of the White House.

Though Douglas—who loved dining out—continued going out to dinner on rare occasions in the months following her appearance at the Medal of Freedom ceremony, she seems to have made no more truly public appearances. Age, quite simply, was doing to Douglas what nothing else ever could. It was forcing her to slow down, to stop "elocuting," to stop fighting. A remarkably active woman her whole life, she was forced to spend much of her time sleeping or just resting at her cottage.

"A lot of reports lead you to believe that she's bright and perky as she always was," said longtime friend Martha Hubbard in April 1996, on Douglas's one hundred and sixth birthday. "She wants to get up and do things and talks about going out and taking you to dinner," Hubbard added. "The spirit is willing but the flesh is weak."[6] Still, when company came calling—especial-

Marjory Stoneman Douglas died at 6:15 A.M. on May 14, 1998. According to a friend, William T. "Toby" Muir, Douglas's nurses were at her bedside when she died. "I'm told she just grew quiet and breathed and crossed her arms over her chest, and with her nurses holding her hand, she quietly slipped away," Muir said. "We should all hope for a passing as graceful and peaceful as that."[7]

Within hours of Douglas's death, environmentalists and politicians around the world responded with praise for her and her life's work. Messages poured in. President Clinton called her a "passionate steward of our nation's natural resources."[8]

Many who spoke of Douglas after her death made note of the fact that the work she started—first with *Everglades, River of Grass*, and then with her stewardship as a public speaker and activist—must be continued.

"The Everglades is not saved. More than ever the Everglades is threatened. We must keep working," said Miami-Dade County Commissioner Katy Sorenson at a special ceremony to honor Douglas not long after her death.[9]

In fact, the Everglades has not been saved. Though the federal government has promised to spend about $8 billion to clean and restore the watershed, there's no guarantee the plans will be carried forward, or that they will be successful in undoing decades of damage.

Meanwhile, in the years since her death, Marjory Stoneman Douglas's life has been further honored. In October 1999, she was inducted into the National

Conservation Hall of Fame. A year later she was induct-ed into the National Women's Hall of Fame.

Douglas's memory will live on. Part of the Everglades itself has been given her name. Her cottage, the tiny house she built in 1926, where she wrote her famous book and from which she waged war to preserve and restore the river of grass, will eventually be turned into a nature and education center known as Glades House.

The greatest tribute to Marjory Stoneman Douglas, however, would be the Everglades itself, safe from harm, restored to at least a semblance of its wild and pristine beauty. Joe Podger, a friend of Douglas's who worked with her for many years, put it simply. "Her gift to us is the Everglades, and what we do with it is our gift to Marjory."[10]

Chapter Notes

Chapter One

1. Robert McClure, "At 106, She's Still Hero of the Everglades," Fort Lauderdale *Sun Sentinel* (April 7, 1996).
2. Al Burt, *Al Burt's Florida* (Tallahassee, FL: University Press of Florida, 1997), p. 135.
3. McClure.
4. McClure.
5. Jeff Klinkenberg, *Real Florida* (Asheboro, NC: Down Home Press, 1993), p. 93.
6. Marjory Stoneman Douglas and John Rothchild, *The Voice of the River* (Sarasota, FL: Pineapple Press, 1987), p. 44.
7. Douglas and Rothchild, p. 45.
8. Douglas and Rothchild, pp. 47–48.
9. Douglas and Rothchild, p. 49.
10. Douglas and Rothchild, p. 43.
11. Douglas and Rothchild, p. 57.

Chapter Two

1. *Taunton High School Journal and Stylus* (Taunton, NJ: 1908), p. 19.
2. *Journal and Stylus*, p. 18.
3. Marjory Stoneman Douglas and John Rothchild, *Voice of the River* (Sarasota, FL: Pineapple Press, 1987), p. 66.
4. *Journal and Stylus*, p. 22.
5. Douglas and Rothchild, p. 69.
6. Douglas and Rothchild, p. 70.

7. Al Burt, *Al Burt's Florida* (Tallahassee, FL: University Press of Florida, 1997), p. 133.
8. Douglas and Rothchild, p. 75.
9. Jean Glasscock, ed., *Wellesley College, 1875–1975: A Century of Women* (Wellesley MA: Wellesley College, 1975), pp. 243–244.
10. Letter, June 27, 1986, Marjory Stoneman Douglas Papers, Miami, FL: Richter Library, University of Miami.
11. Douglas and Rothchild, p. 72.

Chapter Three

1. Marjory Stoneman Douglas and John Rothchild, *Voice of the River* (Sarasota, FL: Pineapple Press, 1987) p. 83.
2. Douglas and Rothchild, p. 83.
3. Douglas and Rothchild, p. 84.
4. Douglas and Rothchild, p. 84.
5. *Certificate and Record of Marriage*, State of New Jersey Bureau of Vital Statistics (April 18, 1914).
6. Douglas and Rothchild, p. 85.
7. Douglas and Rothchild, p. 72.
8. Douglas and Rothchild, p. 88.
9. Douglas and Rothchild, p. 91.
10. Douglas and Rothchild, p. 95.
11. Marjory Stoneman Douglas, *Nine Florida Stories* (Gainesville, FL: Univ. of North Florida Press, 1990), p. 8.

Chapter Four

1. Marjory Stoneman Douglas and John Rothchild, *Voice of the River* (Sarasota, FL: Pineapple Press, 1987), pp. 95–96.
2. Marjory Stoneman Douglas, *Nine Florida Stories* (Gainesville, FL: University of North Florida Press, 1990), p. 5.
3. Douglas and Rothchild, p. 96.
4. Douglas and Rothchild, p. 96.
5. Douglas and Rothchild, p. 96.
6. Douglas and Rothchild, p. 97.
7. Isadore Cohen, *Historical Sketches and Sidelights of Miami, Florida* (Miami: Privately Printed, 1925) pp. 159–160.

8. Douglas and Rothchild, p. 99.
9. Douglas and Rothchild, p. 102.
10. Douglas and Rothchild, p. 103.
11. Daniel Zwerdling, Washington, D.C., *Environmental Matriarch*, "Weekend All Things Considered" (National Public Radio), May 17, 1998.
12. Nancy Ancrum and Rich Bard, eds., *Miami in Our Own Words* (Miami: *The Miami Herald*, 1995), p. 60.

Chapter Five

1. Marjory Stoneman Douglas and John Rothchild, *Voice of the River* (Sarasota, FL: Pineapple Press, 1987), p. 112.
2. R. Z. Sheppard, "Plague of the Century: Tracking the 1918 Flu Virus That Killed 20 Million," (*Time* magazine, December 13, 1999), p. 105.
3. Douglas and Rothchild, p. 115.
4. Douglas and Rothchild, p. 116.
5. Edwin James, *Special to The New York Times*, November 11, 1918, World War I Document Archive, <*http://library.byu. edu/~rdh/wwi/1918/nytend.html*>
6. Douglas and Rothchild, p. 124.
7. Douglas and Rothchild, p. 124.
8. Douglas and Rothchild, p. 126.
9. Douglas and Rothchild, p. 127.
10. Douglas and Rothchild, p. 128.
11. Undated journal entry, 1930, Marjory Stoneman Douglas Papers, Miami, FL: Richter Library, University of Miami.

Chapter Six

1. Undated note, Marjory Stoneman Douglas Papers, Miami, FL: Richter Library, University of Miami.
2. Douglas Papers.
3. Marjory Stoneman Douglas, *The Everglades: River of Grass* (Sarasota, FL: Pineapple Press, 1997), p. 334.
4. Marjory Stoneman Douglas and John Rothschild, *Voice of the River* (Sarasota, FL: Pineapple Press, 1987), p. 128.
5. Douglas and Rothchild, pp. 133–134.
6. Douglas and Rothchild, p. 134.

7. Douglas and Rothchild, p. 166.
8. Douglas and Rothchild, p. 167.
9. Diary entry, August 10, 1924, Marjory Stoneman Douglas Papers, Miami, FL: Richter Library, Univ. of Miami.

Chapter Seven

1. Marjory Stoneman Douglas and John Rothchild, *Voice of the River* (Sarasota, FL: Pineapple Press, 1987), p. 168.
2. Douglas and Rothchild, p. 170.
3. Marjory Stoneman Douglas, *River in Flood and Other Florida Stories* (Gainesville: University Press of Florida, 1998), p. 148.
4. Diary entry, May 1, 1926, Marjory Stoneman Douglas Papers, Miami, FL: Richter Library, University of Miami.
5. Douglas and Rothchild, p. 171.
6. Diary entry, Feb., 1927, Marjory Stoneman Douglas Papers, Miami, FL: Richter Library, University of Miami.
7. Letter, dated January 14, 1930, Marjory Stoneman Douglas Papers, Miami, FL: University of Miami.
8. Douglas and Rothchild, p. 187.
9. Douglas and Rothchild, p. 188.
10. Douglas and Rothchild, p. 189.
11. Undated clipping, *The Miami Herald*, Marjory Stoneman Douglas Papers, Miami, FL: Richter Library, University of Miami.
12. Douglas and Rothchild, p. 190.
13. Douglas and Rothchild, p. 190.

Chapter Eight

1. Marjory Stoneman Douglas, "The Everglades Remembered," *The Florida Naturalist*, (December, 1983), p. 9.
2. Marjory Stoneman Douglas and John Rothschild, *Voice of the River* (Sarasota, FL: Pineapple Press, 1987), p. 190.
3. Jeff Klinkenberg, *Real Florida* (Asheboro, NC: Down Home Press, 1993), p. 90.
4. Douglas and Rothchild, p. 191.
5. Letter, June 11, 1985, Marjory Stoneman Douglas Papers, Miami, FL: Richter Library, University of Miami.
6. Douglas, p. 15.

7. Jim Auchmutey, "Marjory Stoneman Douglas: Champion of the Everglades," *Atlanta Journal and Constitution* (May 15, 1998).
8. Klinkenberg, p. 91.
9. Marjory Stoneman Douglas, *The Everglades: River of Grass* (Sarasota, FL: Pineapple Press, 1997), pp. 5–6.
10. Douglas and Rothchild, p. 190.
11. Douglas, *River of Grass*, p. 8.
12. Douglas, *River of Grass*, p. 17.
13. Douglas, *River of Grass*, p. 18.
14. Douglas, *River of Grass*, pp. 53–54.
15. Auchmutey.
16. Douglas and Rothchild, p. 193
17. Douglas and Rothchild, p. 193.
18. Eliot Kleinberg, "Marjory Stoneman Douglas: April 7, 1890—May 14, 1998: The Voice of the Everglades," *Palm Beach Post* (May 15, 1998).
19. Letter, October 31, 1947, Marjory Stoneman Douglas Papers, Miami, FL: Richter Library, University of Miami.
20. Kleinberg.
21. John Hersey, book review, *New York Herald Tribune* (Nov. 6, 1947), included in Marjory Stoneman Douglas Papers, Miami, FL: Richter Library, University of Miami.
22. Klinkenberg, p. 91.

Chapter Nine

1. Marjory Stoneman Douglas and John Rothchild, *Voice of the River* (Sarasota, FL: Pineapple Press, 1987), p. 202.
2. Diary, 1947, Marjory Stoneman Douglas Papers, Miami, FL: University of Miami.
3. Douglas and Rothchild, p. 202.
4. Douglas and Rothchild, p. 203.
5. Robert McClure, "At 106, She's Still Hero of the Everglades," Fort Lauderdale *Sun Sentinel* (April 7, 1996).
6. McClure.
7. Margaria Fichtner, "Marjory Stoneman Douglas," *The Miami Herald* (September 22, 1985).
8. Margaria Fichtner, "Landscapes and Letters," *The Miami Herald* (April 7, 1983).
9. Fichtner, "Marjory Stoneman Douglas."
10. Al Burt, "The Elocutioner," *The Miami Herald* (March 18, 1984).
11. Marjory Stoneman Douglas letter, July 18, 1985, Marjory Stoneman Douglas Papers, Miami, FL: University of Miami.

12. Marjory Stoneman Douglas letter.
13. "Obituary of Marjory Stoneman Douglas," *London Daily Telegraph* (May 20, 1998).
14. Associated Press, "Crusader Fights for 'Glades, *The Bradenton Herald*, March 31, 1996.
15. Jeff Klinkenberg, *Real Florida* (Asheboro, NC: Down Home Press, 1993), p. 93.
16. Jim Auchmutey, "Marjory Stoneman Douglas, Champion of the Everglades: Florida Environmentalist Dies at 108," *Atlanta Journal and Constitution* (May 15, 1998).

Chapter Ten

1. <ABCNews.com>
2. Staff Writers, "Everglades' Hero Turns 105," *Palm Beach Post* (April 8, 1995).
3. Associated Press, "Everglades 'Grandmother' Douglas Turns 106," *Palm Beach Post* (April 8, 1996).
4. Donna Gehrke, "Champion of Everglades Turns 107," *Miami Herald* (April 7, 1997).
5. Larry Lipman, "Everglades Author Honored by Clinton," *Palm Beach Post* (December 1, 1993).
6. Associated Press.
7. Eliot Kleinberg, "Marjory Stoneman Douglas: April 7, 1890-May 14, 1998: The Voice of the Everglades," *Palm Beach Post* (May 15, 1998).
8. Richard Severo, "Marjory Douglas, Champion of Everglades, Dies at 108," *The New York Times* (May 15, 1998).
9. Scott Hiaasen, "Everglades Is Site of Tribute to Marjory Stoneman Douglas," *Palm Beach Post* (May 24, 1998).
10. Hiaasen.

Bibliography

Primary Sources

Douglas, Marjory with John Rothchild. *Voice of the River*. Sarasota, FL: Pineapple Press, 1987.

Douglas, Marjory Stoneman. *The Everglades: River of Grass*. Sarasota, FL: Pineapple Press, 1997.

Douglas, Marjory Stoneman. *Nine Florida Stories*. Jacksonville, FL: University of North Florida Press, 1990.

Douglas, Marjory Stoneman. *River in Flood and Other Florida Stories*. Gainesville, FL: University Press of Florida, 1998.

Douglas, Marjory Stoneman. *Marjory Stoneman Douglas Papers*. Miami, FL: Otto Richter Library, University of Miami.

Selected Secondary Sources

Ancrum, Nancy and Rich Bard, Editors. *Miami In Our Own Words*. Miami, FL: *The Miami Herald*, 1995.

Burt, Al. *Al Burt's Florida*. Tallahassee, FL: University Press of Florida, 1997.

Chandler, David Leon. *Henry Flagler*. New York: Macmillan, 1986.

Cohen, Isadore. *Historical Sketches and Sidelights of Miami, Florida*. Miami, FL: Privately Printed, 1925.

Derr, Mark. *Some Kind of Paradise*. Tallahassee, FL: University Press of Florida, 1998.

Frazure, Hoyt as told to Nixon Smiley. *Memories of Old Miami*. Miami, FL: *Miami Herald*, (Undated Reprint).

Glasscock, Jean, General Editor. *Wellesley College, 1875–1975: A Century of Women*. Wellesley, MA: Wellesley College, 1975.

Klinkenberg, Jeff. *Real Florida*. Asheboro, NC: Down Home Press, 1993.

Smiley, Nixon. *Yesterday's Miami*. Miami, FL: E.A. Seemann Publishing, 1973.

Taunton High School Journal and Stylus. Taunton, NJ: 1908.

Tebeau, Charlton. *A History of Florida*. Miami, FL: University of Miami Press, 1971.

Newspapers/Magazines

Atlanta Journal and Constitution, May 15, 1998.

The Bradenton Herald, March 31, 1996.

The Miami Herald, April 7, 1983; March 18, 1984; September 22, 1985; April 7, 1997.

The Florida Naturalist, December, 1983.

Fort Lauderdale *Sun Sentinel*, April 7, 1996.

New York Herald Tribune, November 6, 1947.

The New York Times, November 11, 1918; May 15, 1998.

Palm Beach Post, December 1, 1993; April 8, 1995; April 8, 1996; May 15, 1998; May 24, 1998.

Time, December 13, 1999.

Index

About the Author

Kieran Doherty has had a long
career as a writer of nonfiction,
including ten books, but only turned
his attention to writing for young
adults about five years ago. Previous
books for The Millbrook Press and
Twenty-First Century Books include
biographies of colonists William Penn,
William Bradford, and Captain John
Smith. Kieran Doherty lives with his
wife in Lake Worth, Florida.

DATE DUE

Demco, Inc. 38-293